TERMINATRIX
THE SARAH PALIN CHRONICLES

COMPILED BY THE EDITORS OF THE WASILLA IRON DOG GAZETTE

Collins
An Imprint of HarperCollins*Publishers*

TERMINATRIX. Copyright © 2008 by HarperCollins Publishers. All rights reserved. Printed in the United States of America. No part of this book may be used or reproduced in any manner whatsoever without written permission except in the case of brief quotations embodied in critical articles and reviews. For information, address HarperCollins Publishers, 10 East 53rd Street, New York, NY 10022.

HarperCollins books may be purchased for educational, business, or sales promotional use. For information, please write: Special Markets Department, HarperCollins Publishers, 10 East 53rd Street, New York, NY 10022.

FIRST EDITION

Design and photoshopping by James L. Iacobelli

ISBN: 978-0-06-177872-8

08 09 10 11 12 /RRD   10 9 8 7 6 5 4 3 2 1

Everything asserted in the text and photos of this book is absolutely true, with no alteration of any primary source material whatsoever. And Alaska is a great place to work on your winter tan.

The surprise nomination of Alaska Gov. Sarah Palin as John McCain's vice-presidential running mate has rocked the country—and the world. Rumors flood the media and reporters from every major news organization have descended en masse on tiny Wasilla, Alaska, demanding to know, "Who is the real Sarah Palin? Is she really the dynamic straight-talking, gun-toting, corruption-fighting, omni-capable mother of five her supporters claim she is? What qualifications does she have for national office? What foreign policy experience qualifies her to succeed John McCain as president?"

We, the editors of the *Wasilla Iron Dog Gazette,* have known Sarah Palin all her life—as a teenage basketball star, a beauty queen, a city council member, mayor, governor, and now vice-presidential candidate—and so much more. The stories that have circulated previously about her barely scratch the surface. Indeed, if we wrote down everything we know, you probably wouldn't believe us. However, thanks to tireless investigative work and access to a crucial source close to the Governor, we have managed to obtain a private collection of family photos, published here for the first time. Some of them are annotated in the Governor's own hand, providing a fascinating running commentary on her life.

Who is the real Sarah Palin? Yes, she is a hockey mom with an extraordinary political story. But she is much, much more than that.

—The Editors

Sarah's great-great-great-great-grandmother Chastity Louise was among those who came to this country in search of religious freedom.

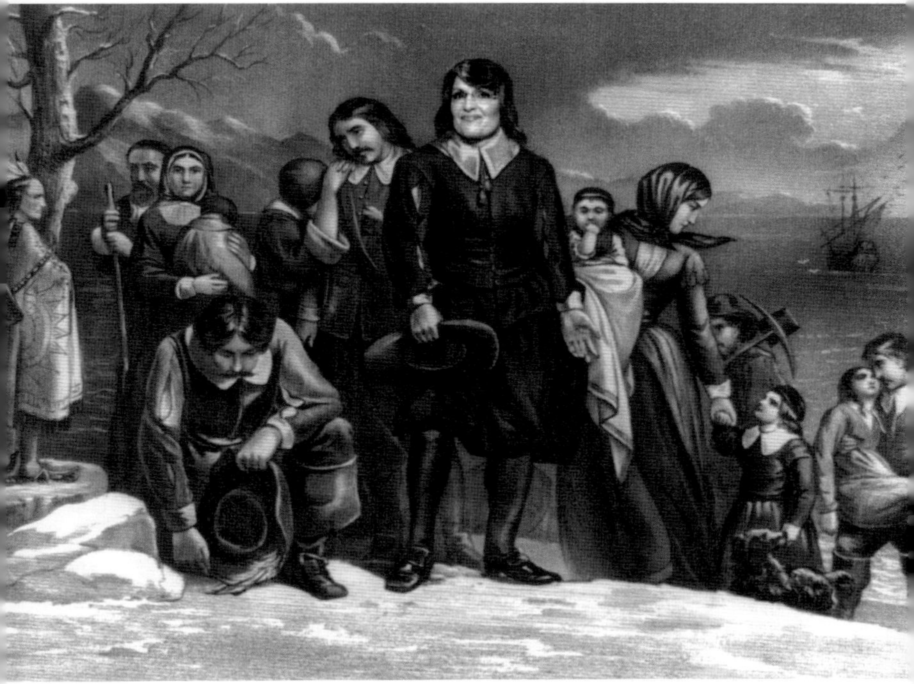

Even as a baby, Sarah Palin came out swinging. Here, in an undated photograph from the mid-'60s, she is seen training for an upcoming bout with heavyweight champ Sonny Liston.

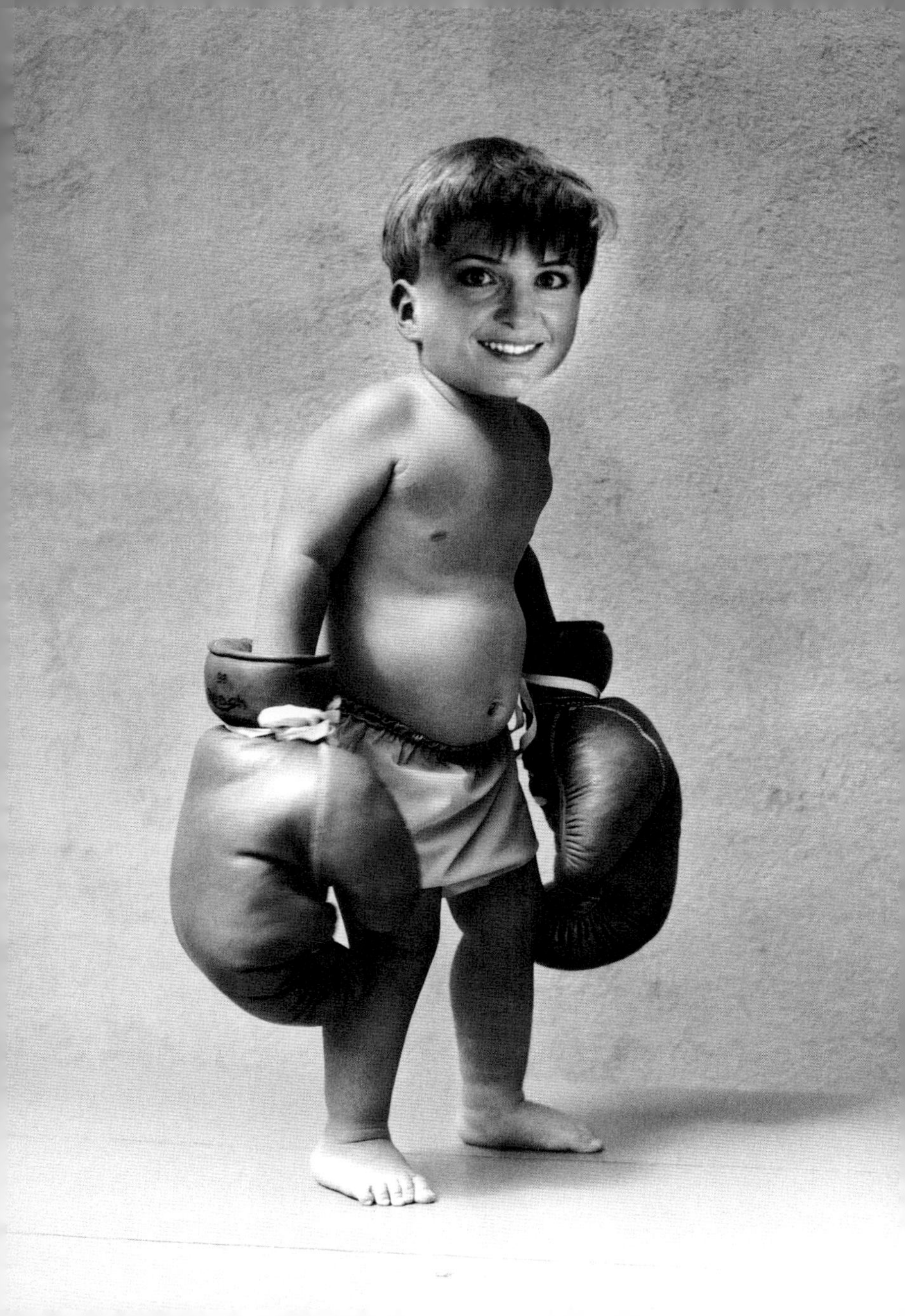

Sarah's was a typically carefree youth, full of trips to the ol' fishing hole with Tom Sawyer or rafting down the Mississippi with a runaway slave named Jim.

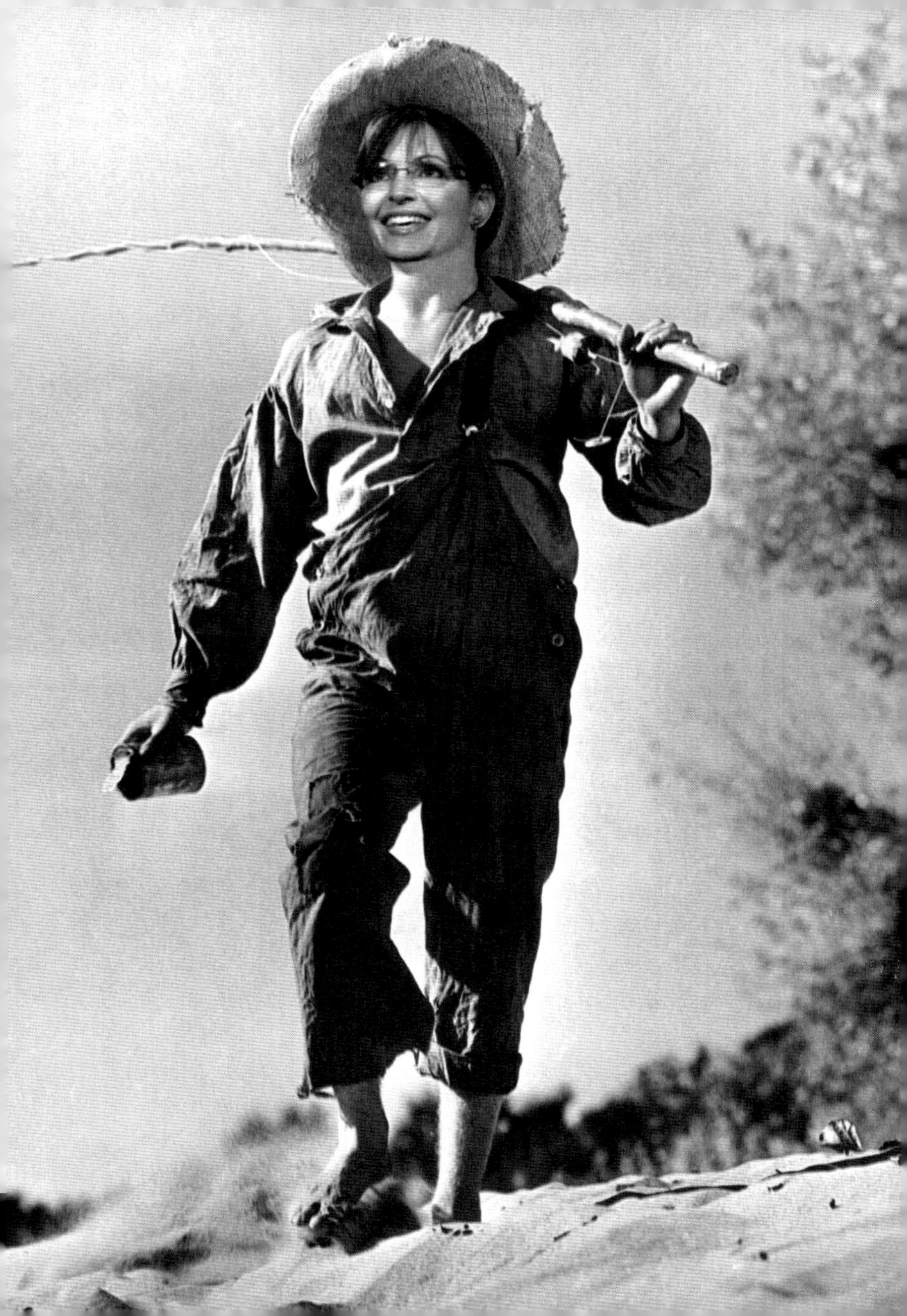

Sarah's deep love of country is bred in her bones.
Here she is as Lady Liberty in her eighth-grade play.

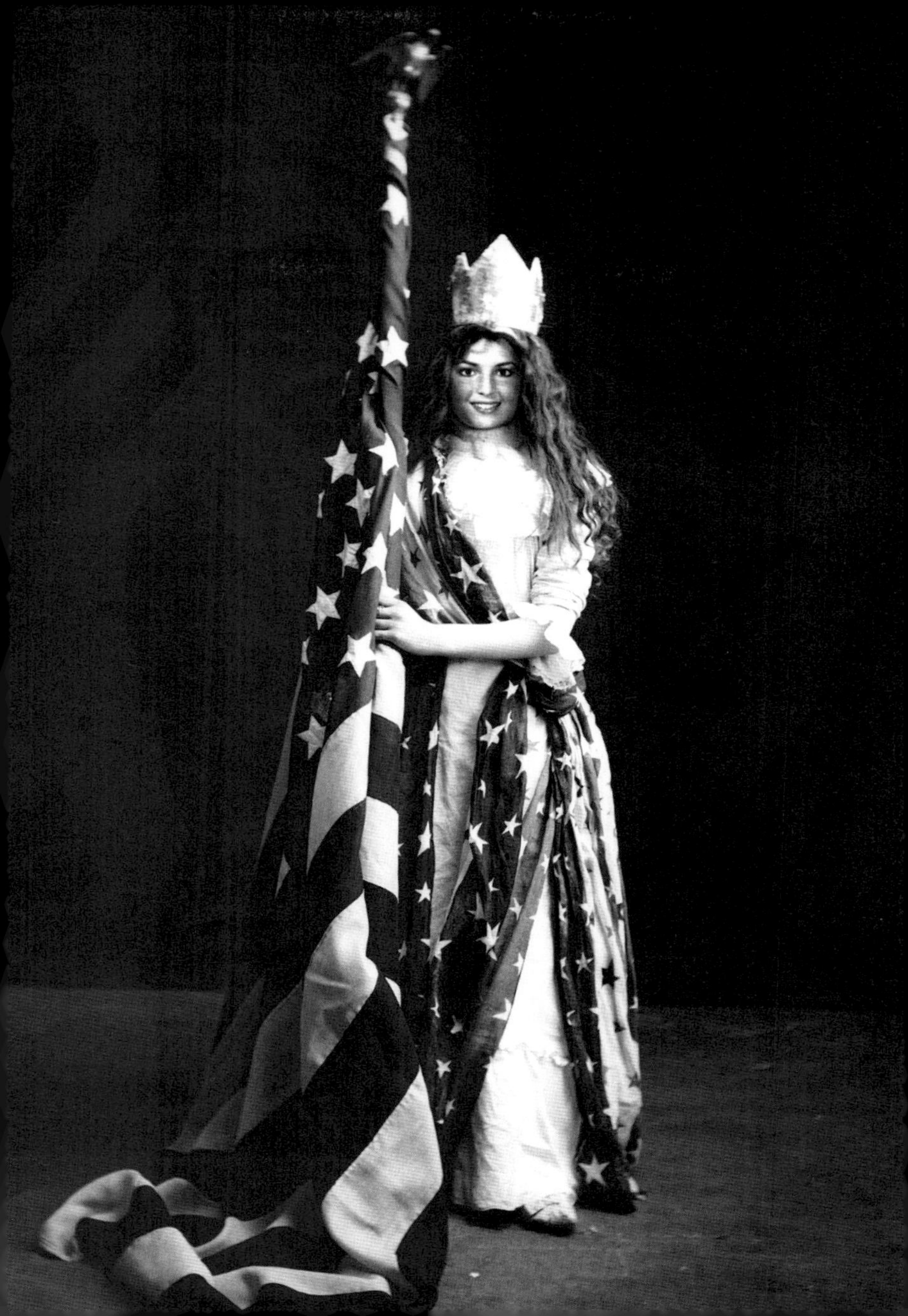

"Some of my fondest childhood memories involve learning to sew from my mom."

BETSEY ROSS

Sarah learned to shoot at a young age and often went hunting with her dad. Here she is posing with her sharpshooting medals.

COPYRIGHT 1899
RICHARD K. FOX

Frontier life teaches hard work and self-reliance. Here is teenaged Sarah splitting rails on her family's farm.

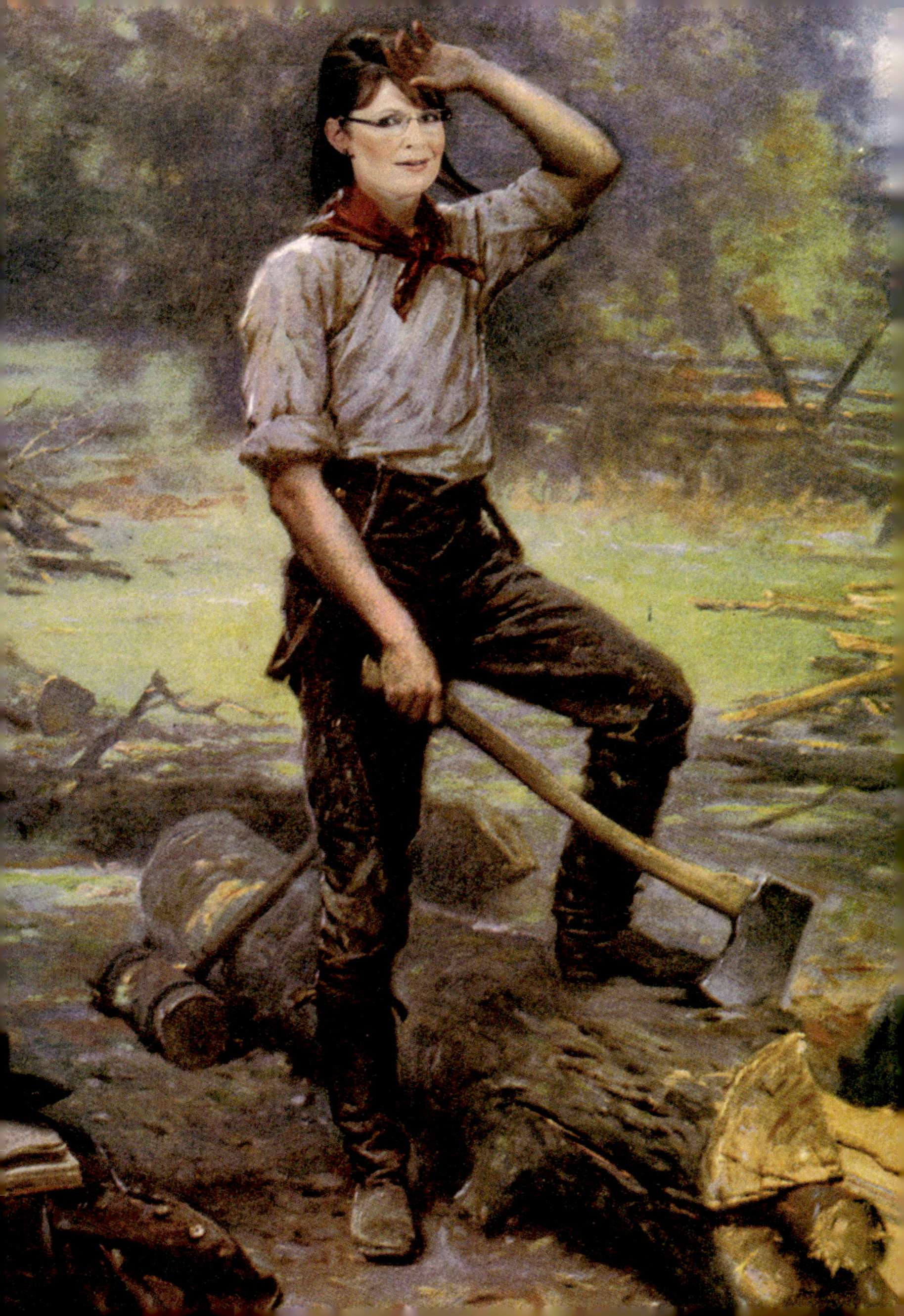

On her parents' remote wilderness homestead, formal education was not an option, so Sarah was homeschooled. Here she is reading by firelight after finishing the day's chores.

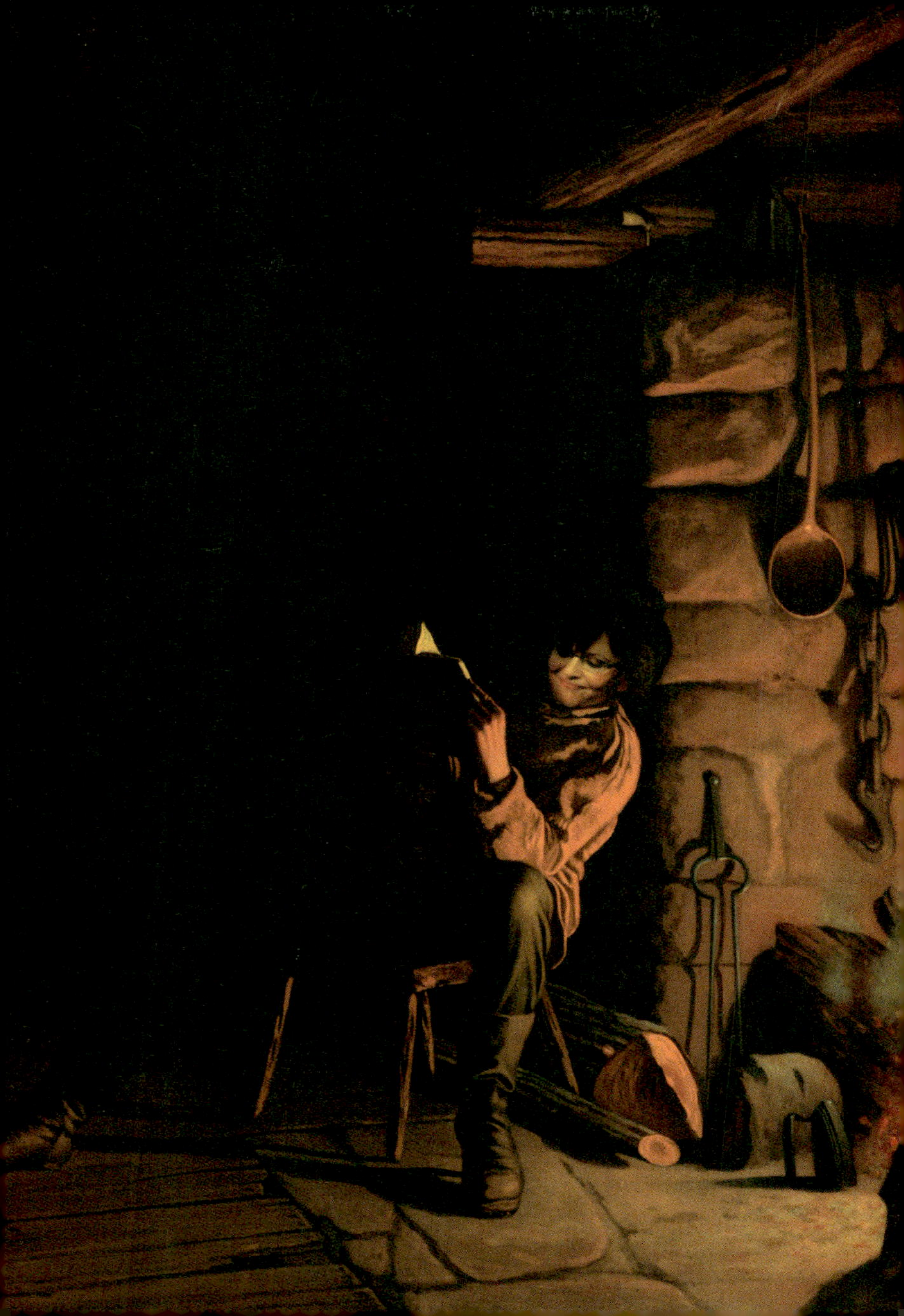

In between junior high and high school, Sarah heard God's call to save France.

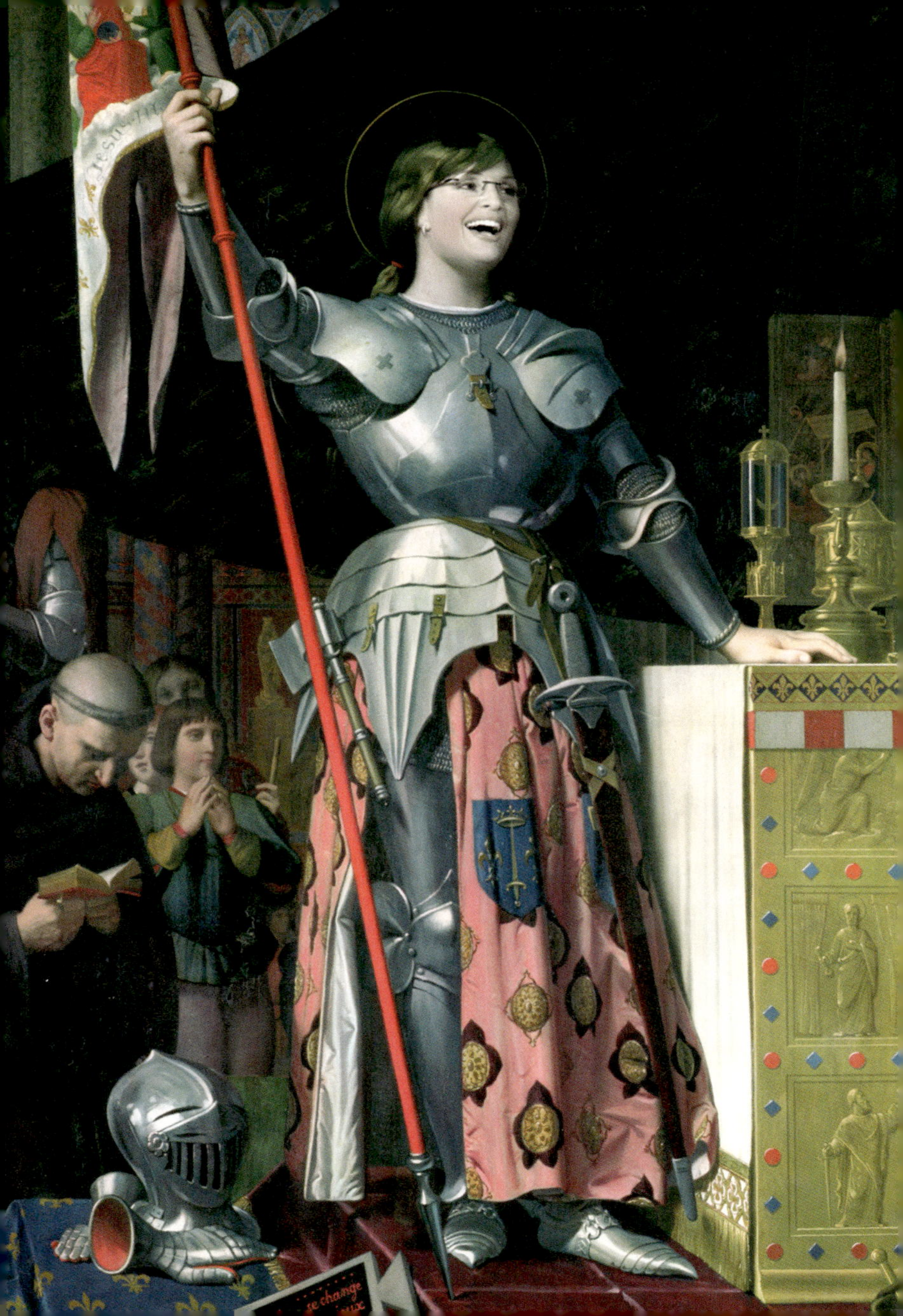

Even as the Framers struggled to draft our founding document, the forces of corruption and politics-as-usual threatened to derail the American experiment. Sarah selflessly put her career and family life on hold to bring much-needed reform to Philadelphia.

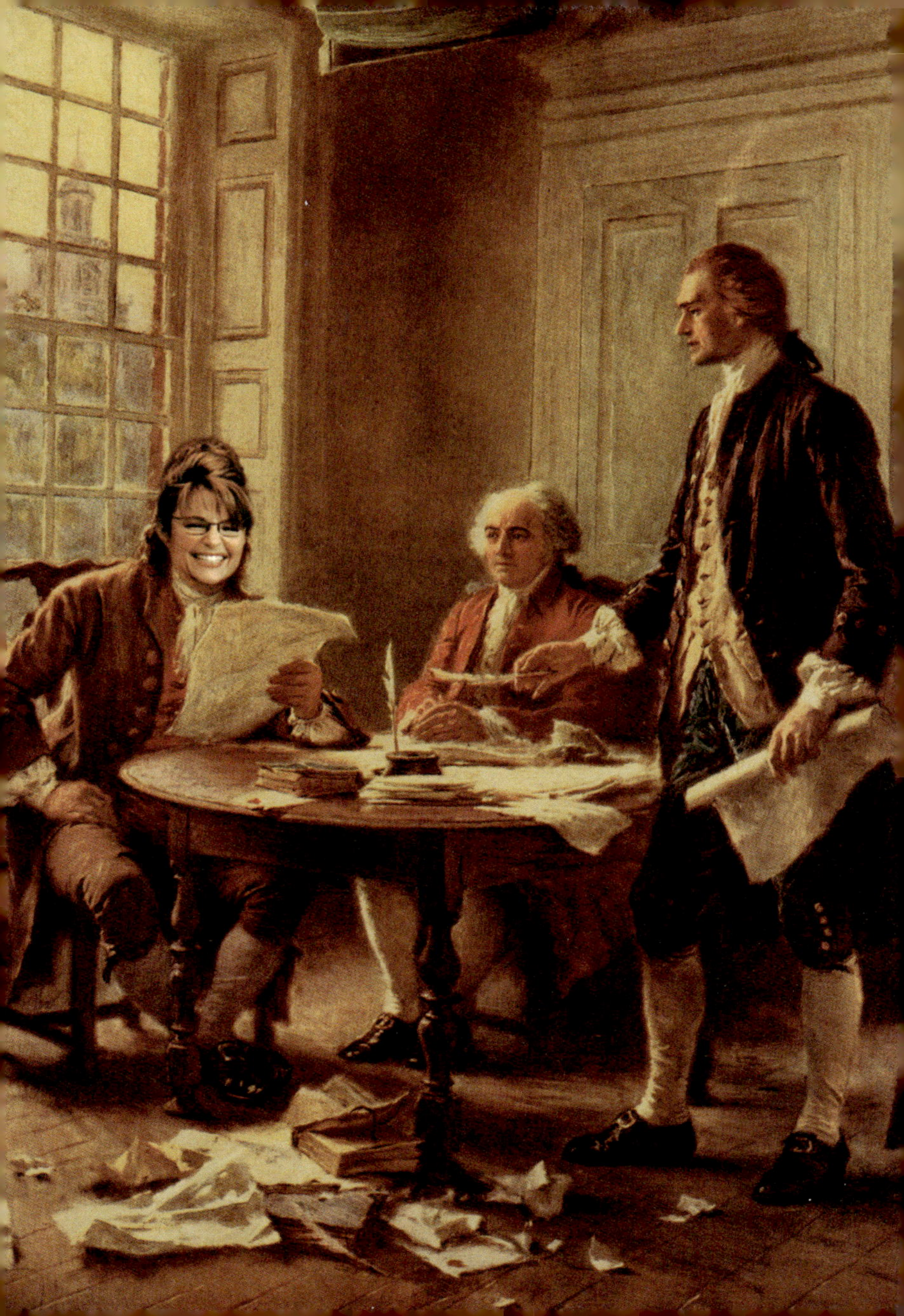

Someone had to open the West for early settlers. With her buckskins and trusty flintlock, Sarah blazed a trail through the Cumberland Gap.

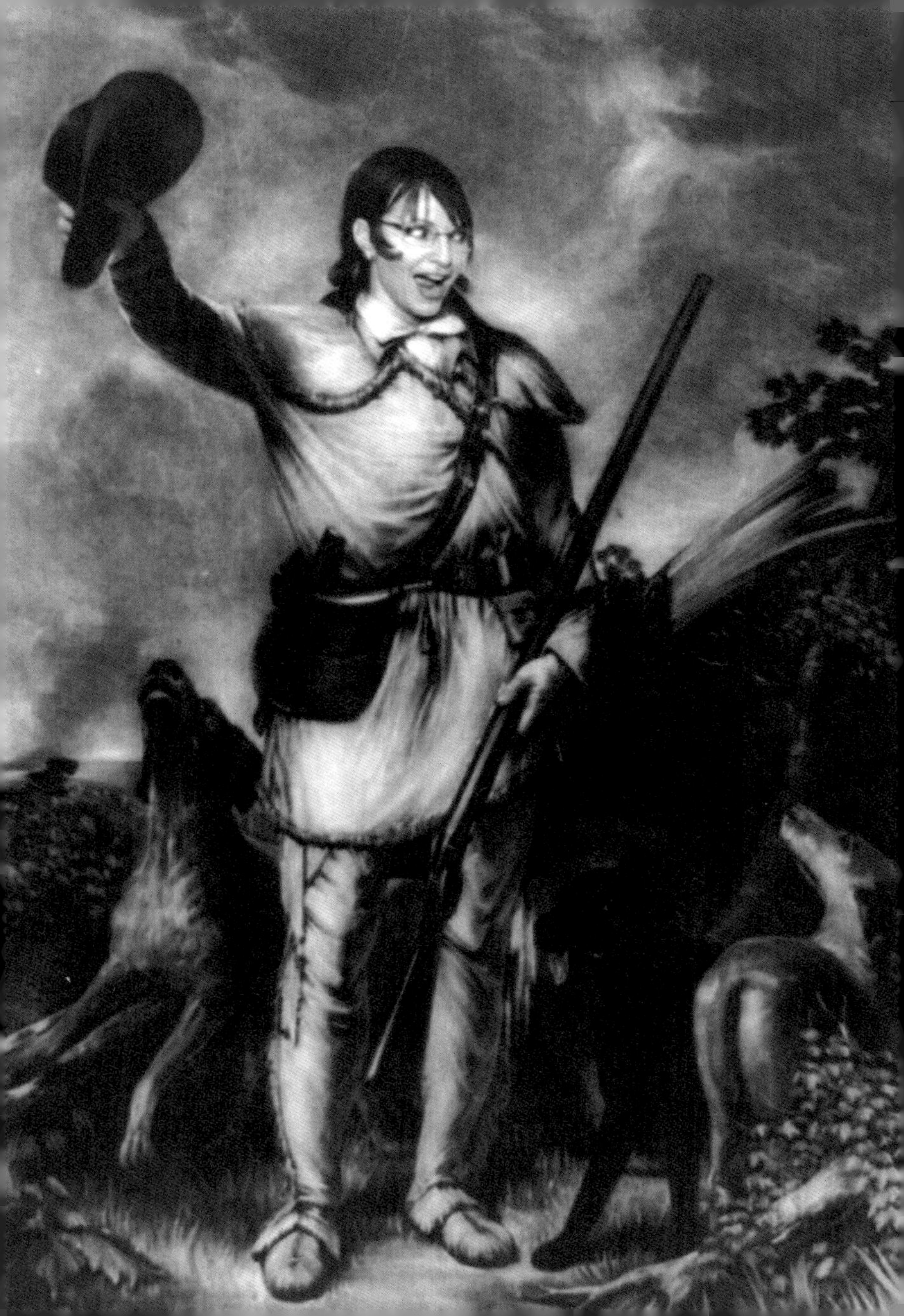

"This is me in shop class building a 12-cylinder engine for my first dirt bike. Boy, could that baby fly!"

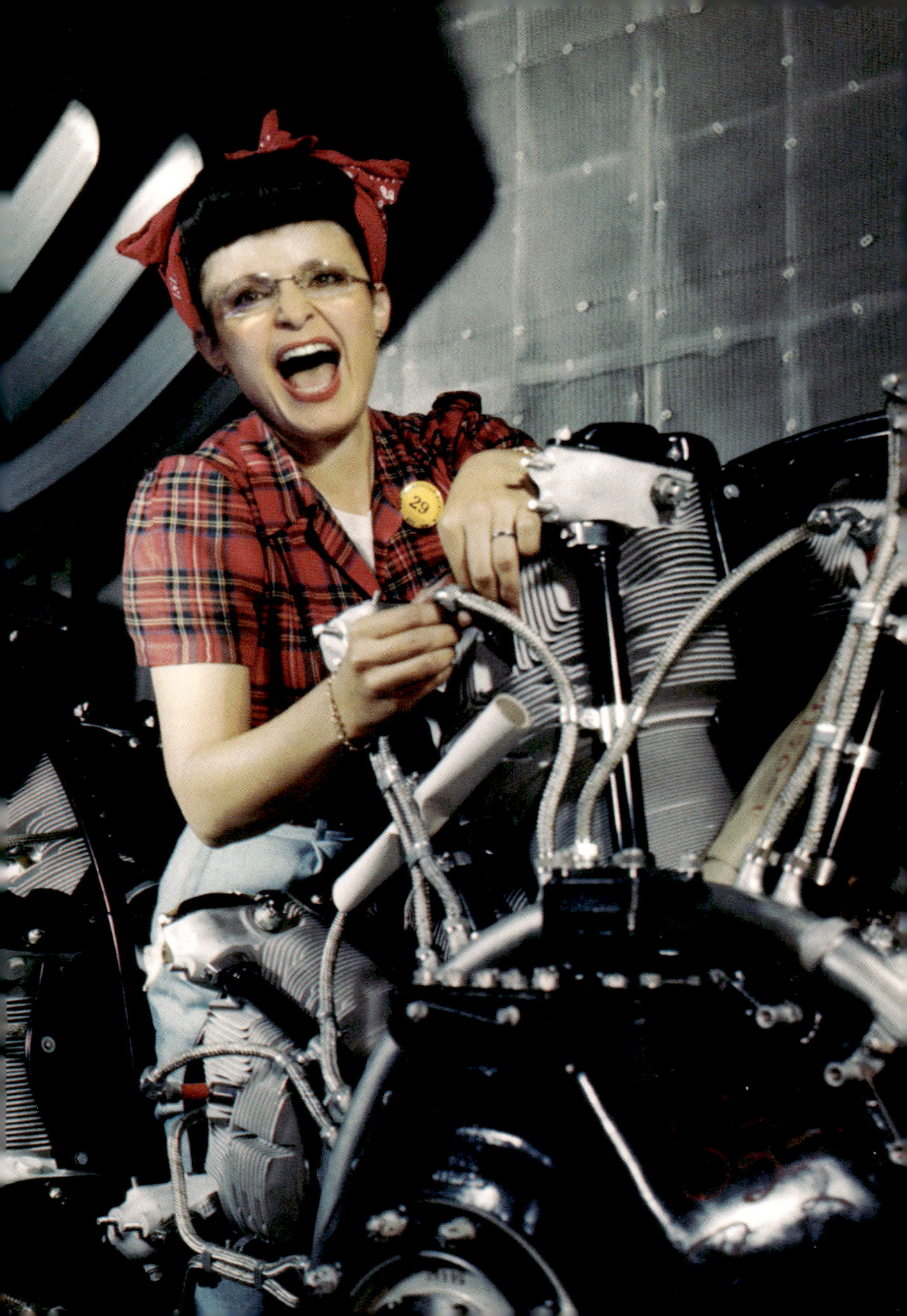
29

"Sarah Barracuda" carried her high school basketball team to victory in the state championship in 1982, sinking a crucial free throw despite a fractured ankle. She also led the team in prayer before games.

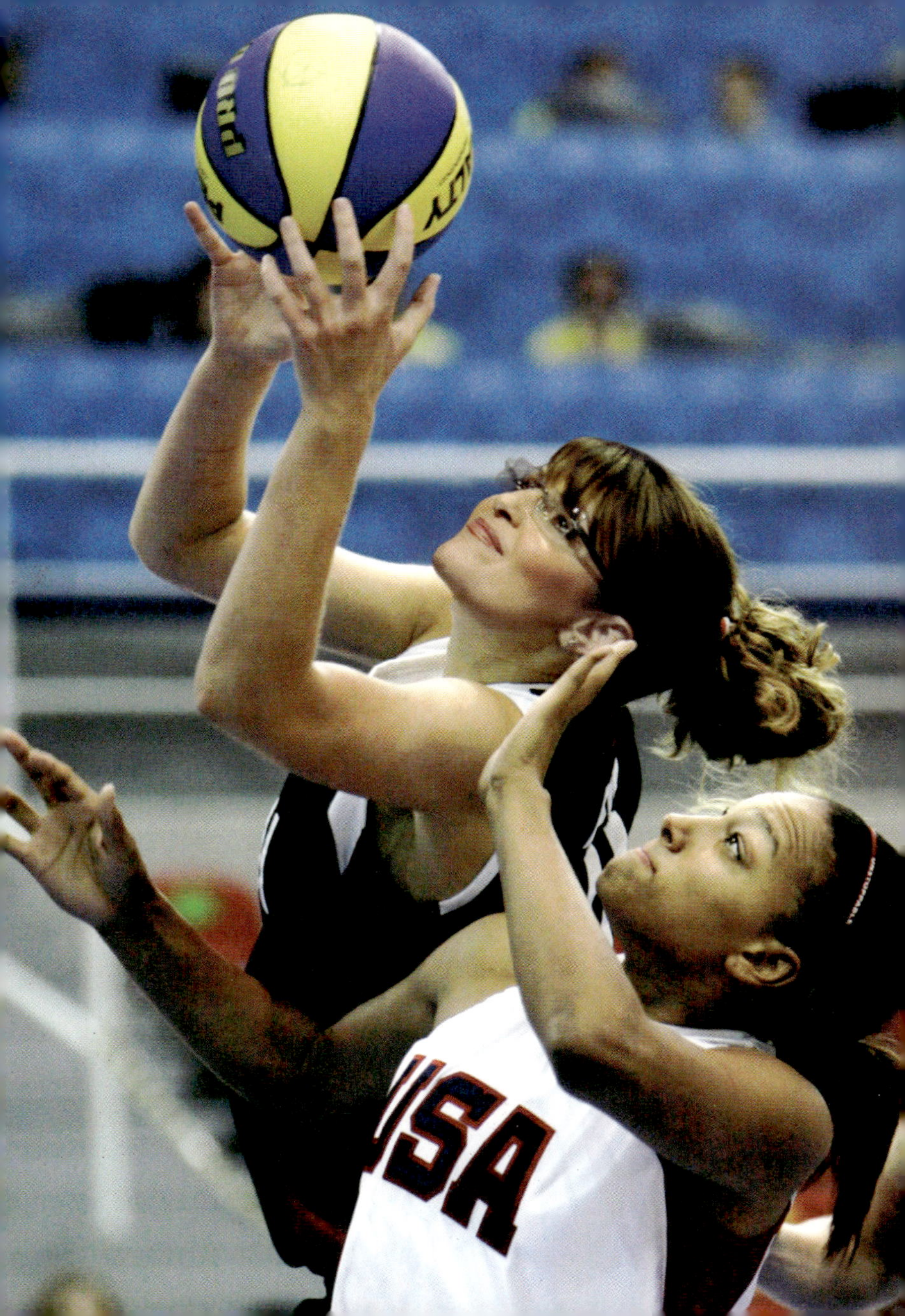
USA

Beginning in her teens, Sarah trained seriously in martial arts, earning her black belt under the legendary Sonny Chiba.

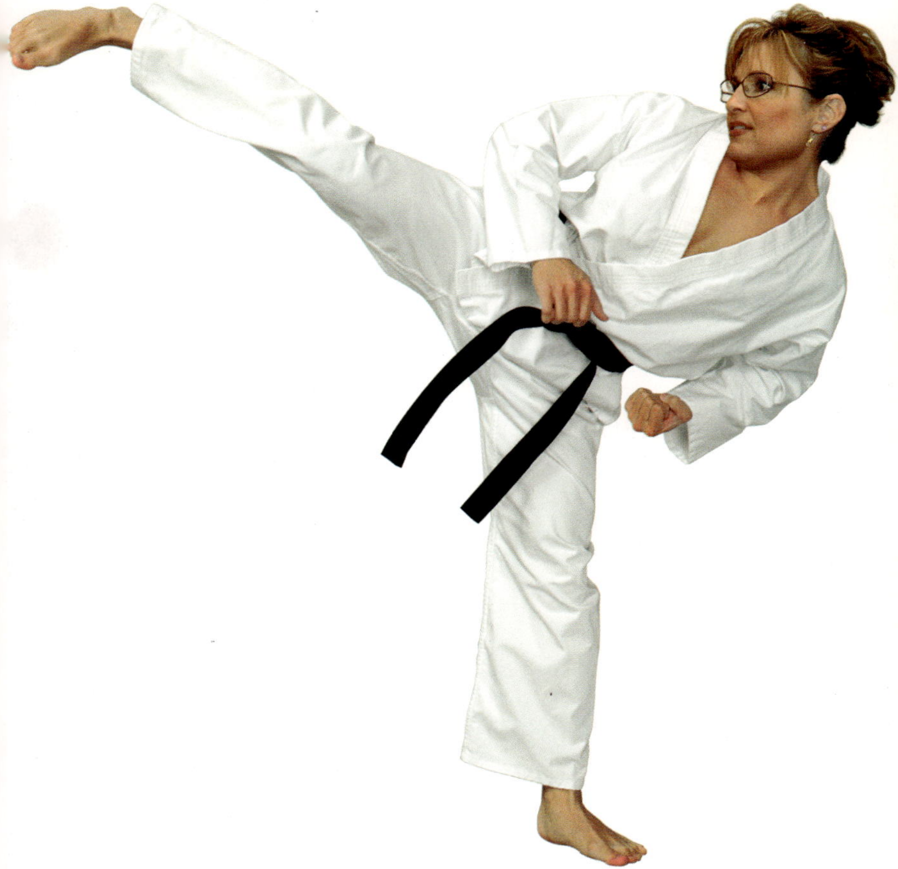

Dreams of yellow ore drove many settlers into the Alaskan wilderness, and Sarah's family was no exception. After a hard journey across the plains in covered wagons, fighting hunger, thirst, and Indian attacks, they finally reached the Yukon. Here is a rare photo of Sarah panning for gold during her summer vacation, before her senior year of college.

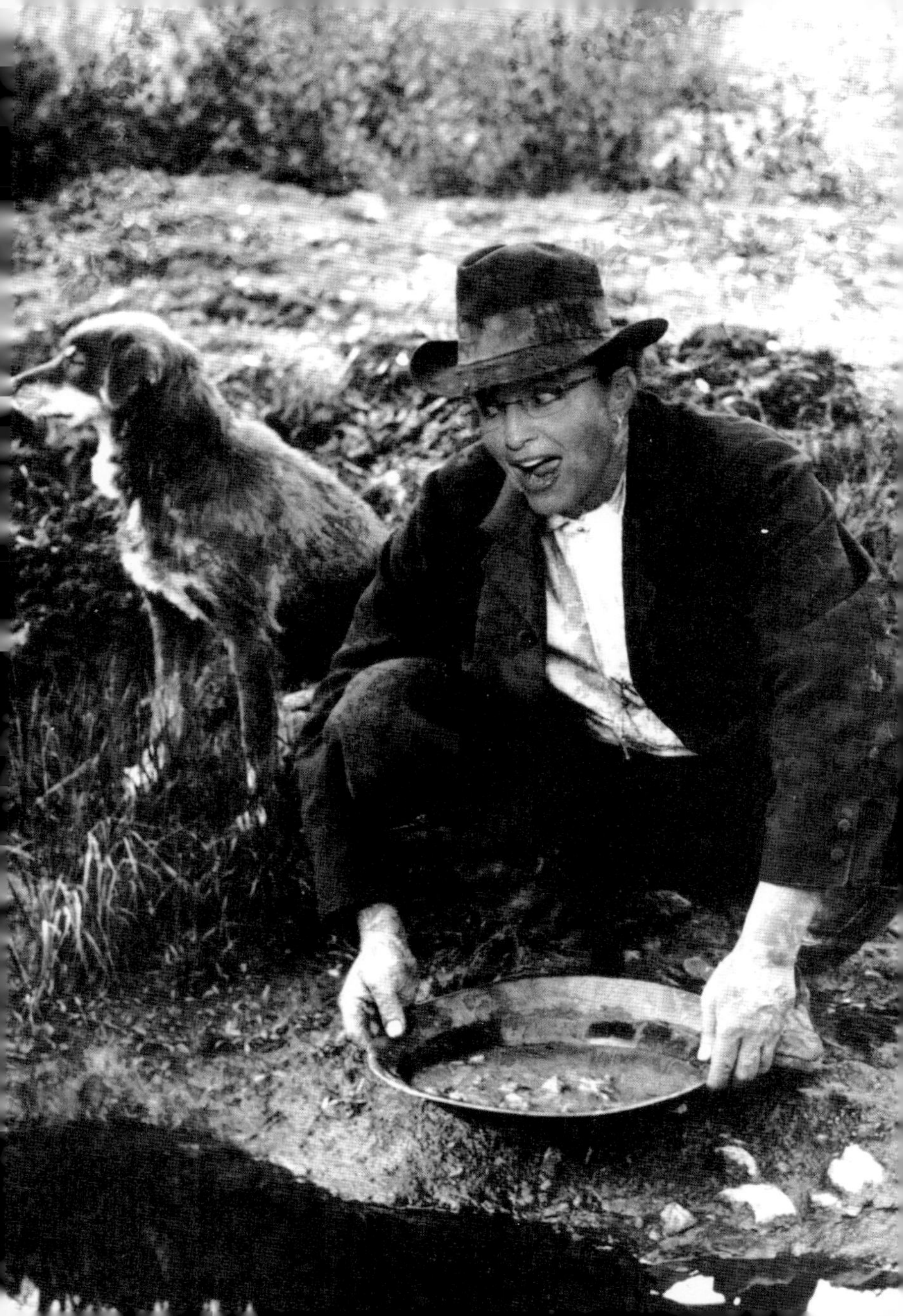

Sarah Palin won the Miss Wasilla Pageant in 1984, while in college.

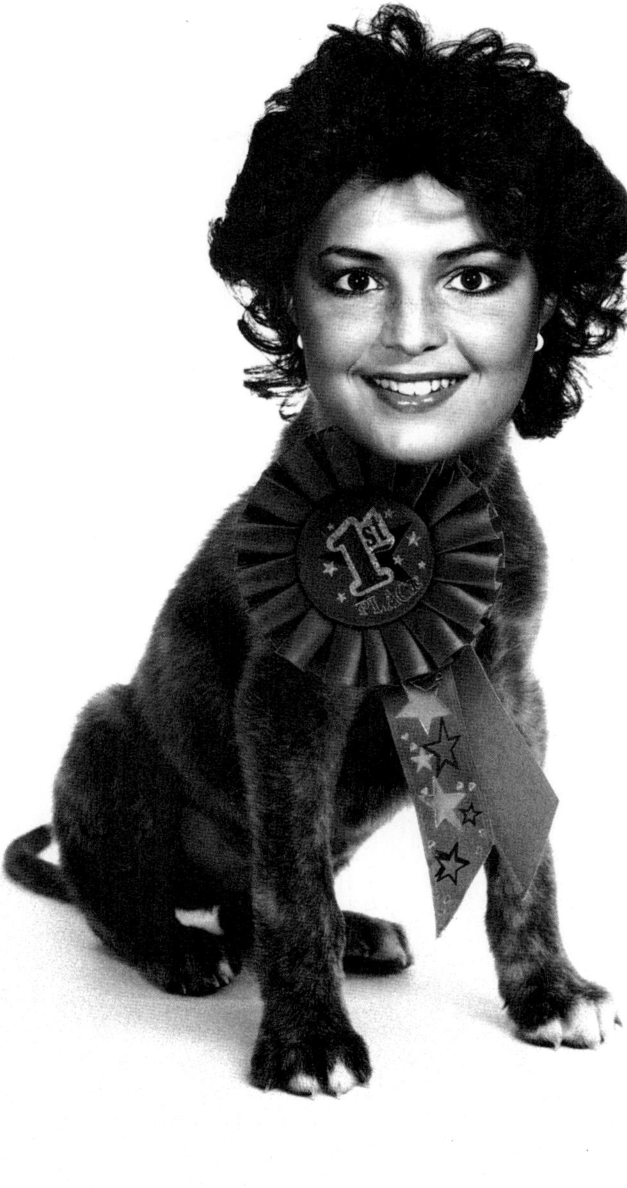
1st

Unlike other conservatives who merely boast of their affinity with Teddy Roosevelt, Sarah actually knew the Rough Rider. After he broke his glasses at San Juan Hill, she stepped in and led the famous charge in his stead.

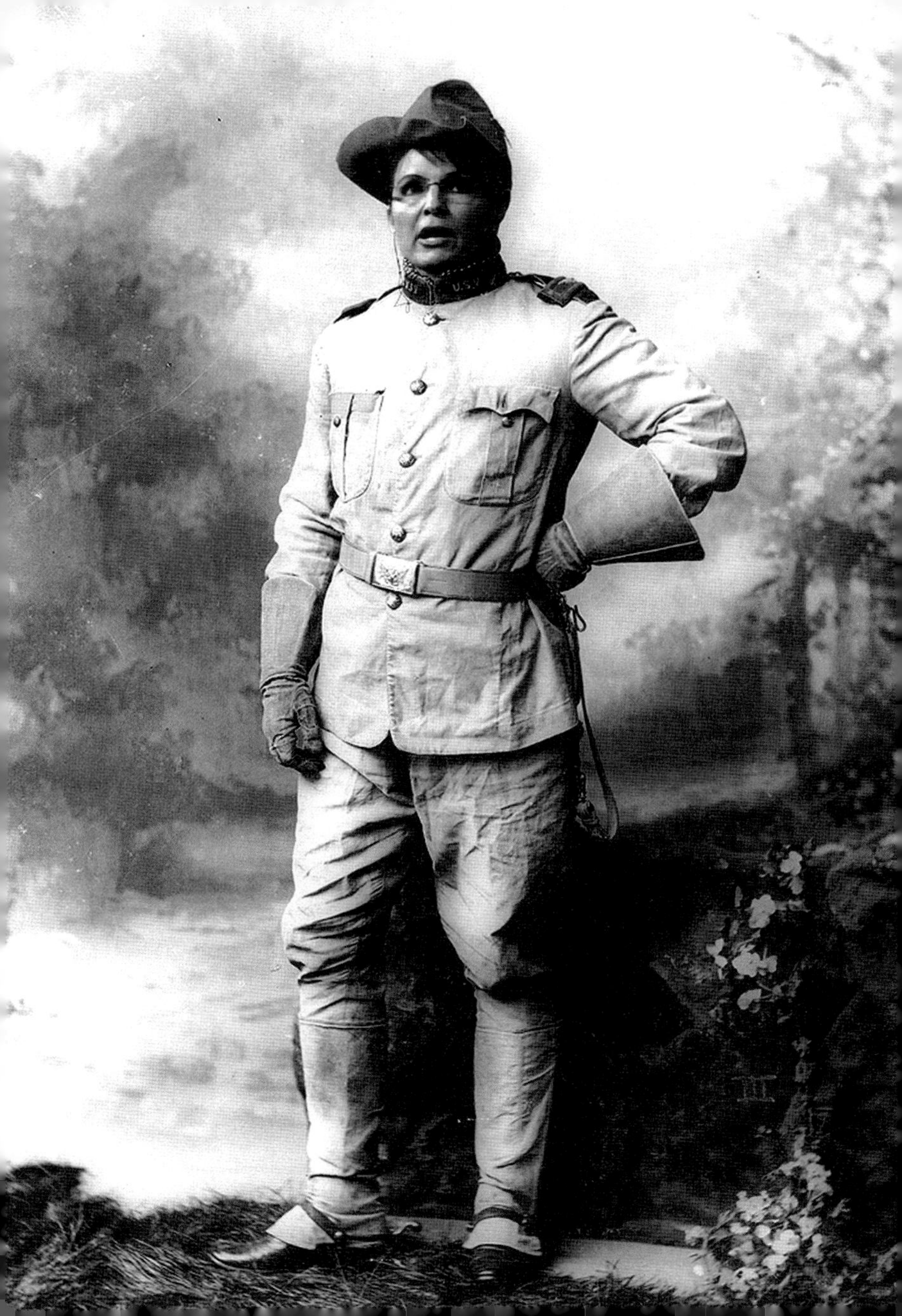

When John Scopes landed in a courtroom for violating a Tennessee statute making it unlawful to teach the theory of evolution in a state-funded school, the case made national headlines. Here, Sarah faces off against famed civil rights lawyer Clarence Darrow, arguing the case against Darwin's godless theory.

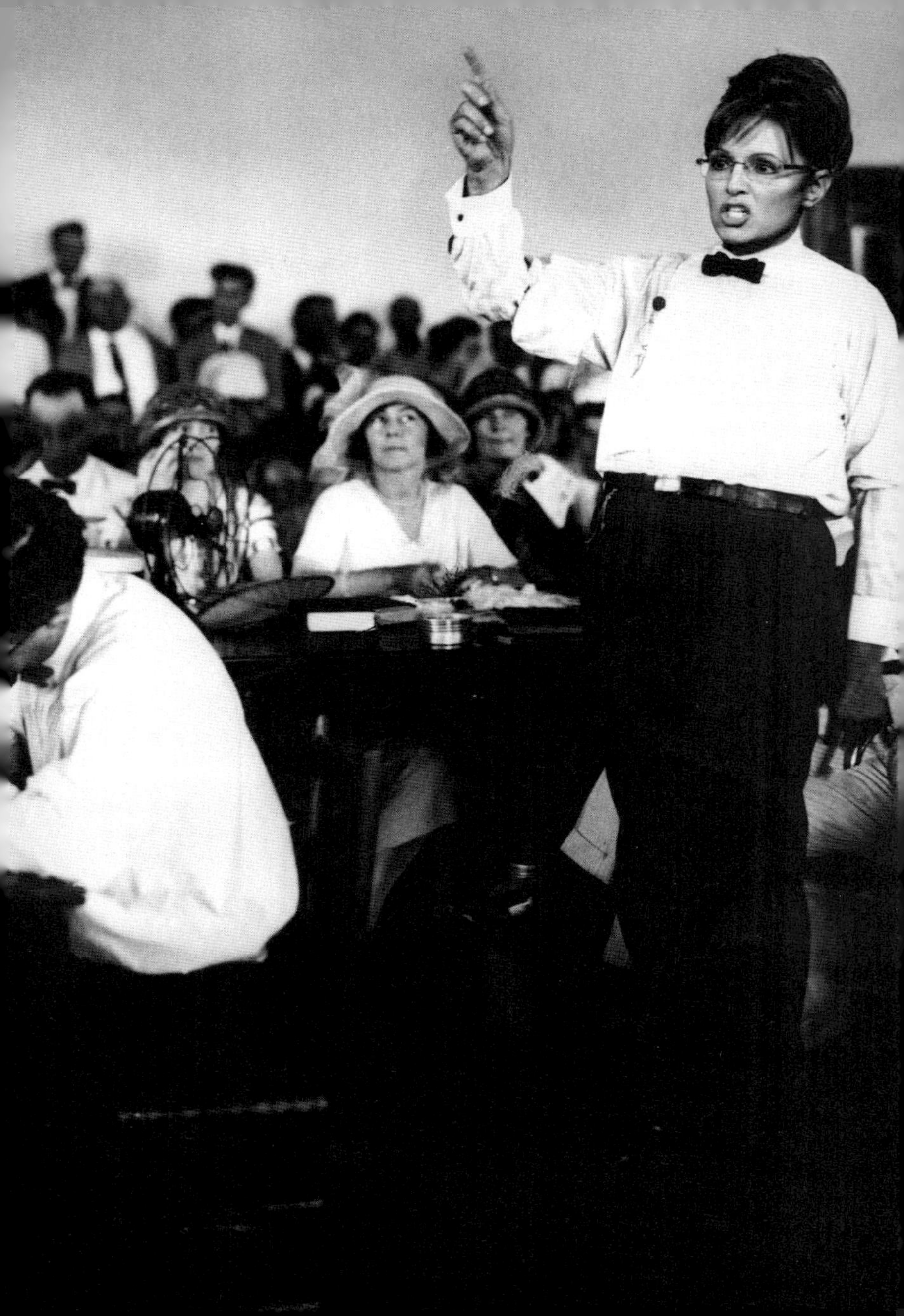

Even before the start of her political career, Palin proved to be a pioneer in bringing equality to women in the workplace.

I'm Proud... my husband wants me to do my part

SEE YOUR U. S. EMPLOYMENT SERVICE
WAR MANPOWER COMMISSION

Sarah has a long record of government service at the highest levels and has served many presidents as an advisor and speechwriter. Here she works over a draft of his inaugural address with President-elect John F. Kennedy. (Ted Sorensen was on vacation.)

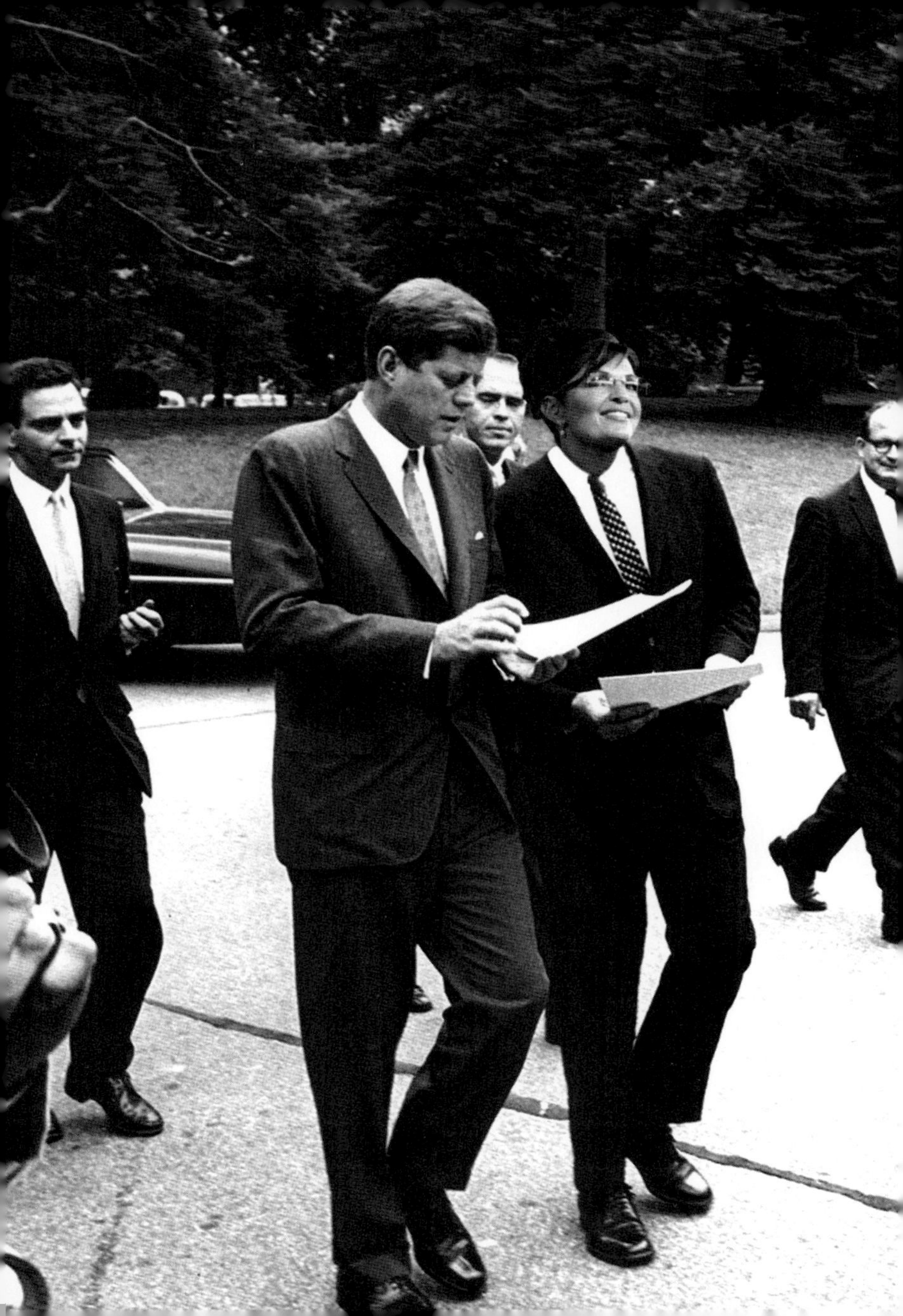

"This is me and Todd on our honeymoon. Isn't he a handsome devil?"

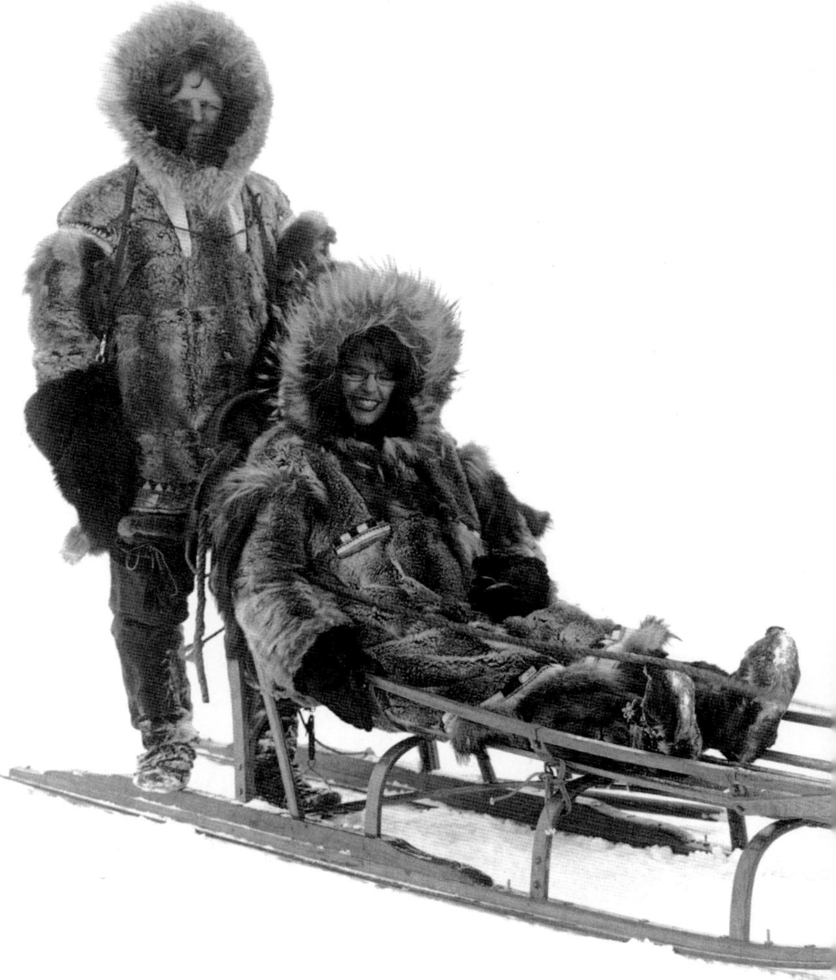

Sarah is a perfectionist in everything she does. Here she is showing off her pecs for the cover of *Yukon Muscle Babe*.

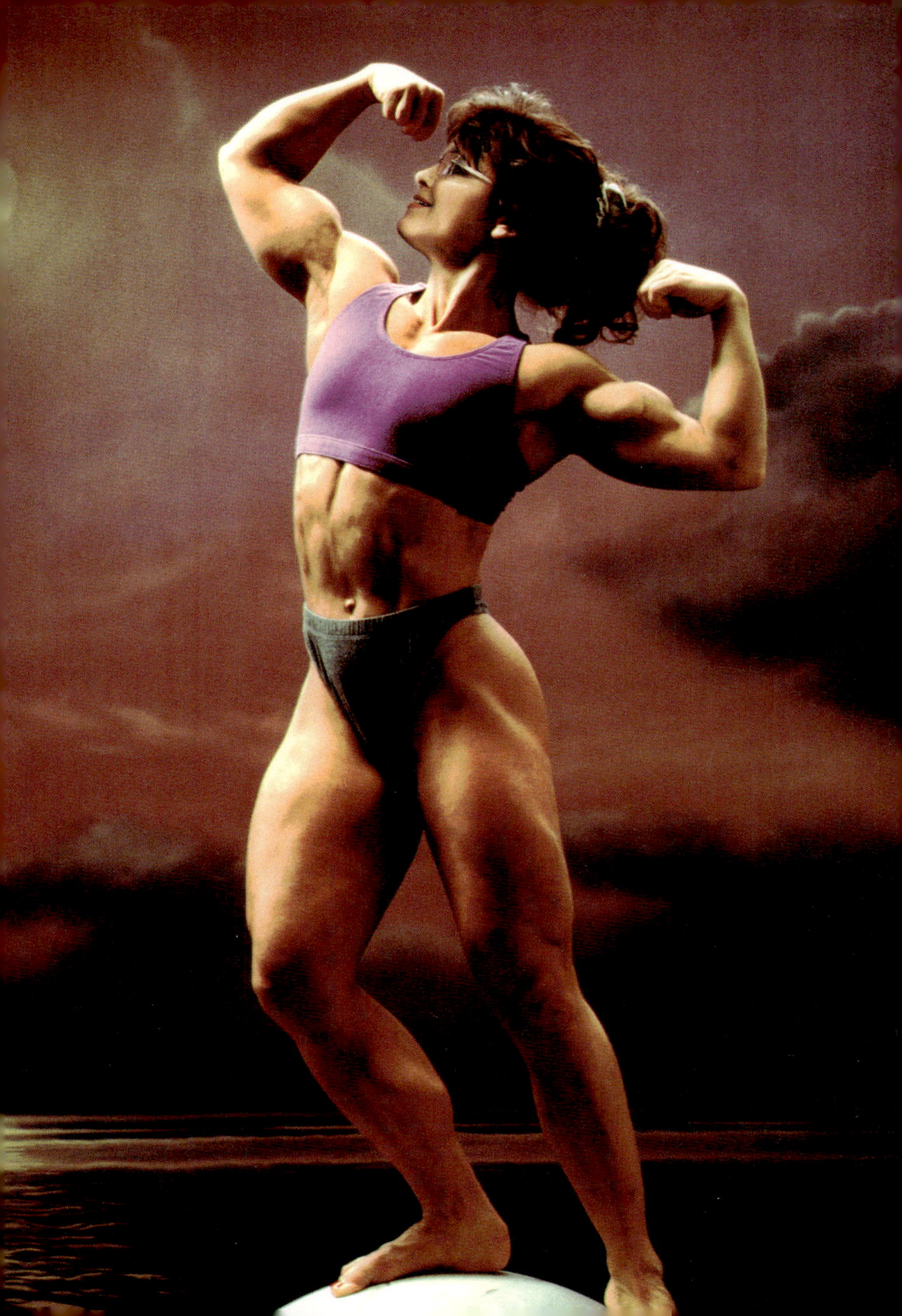

"This is a shot of me with my weight lifting coach and political mentor. Despite the rumors, we never actually dated."

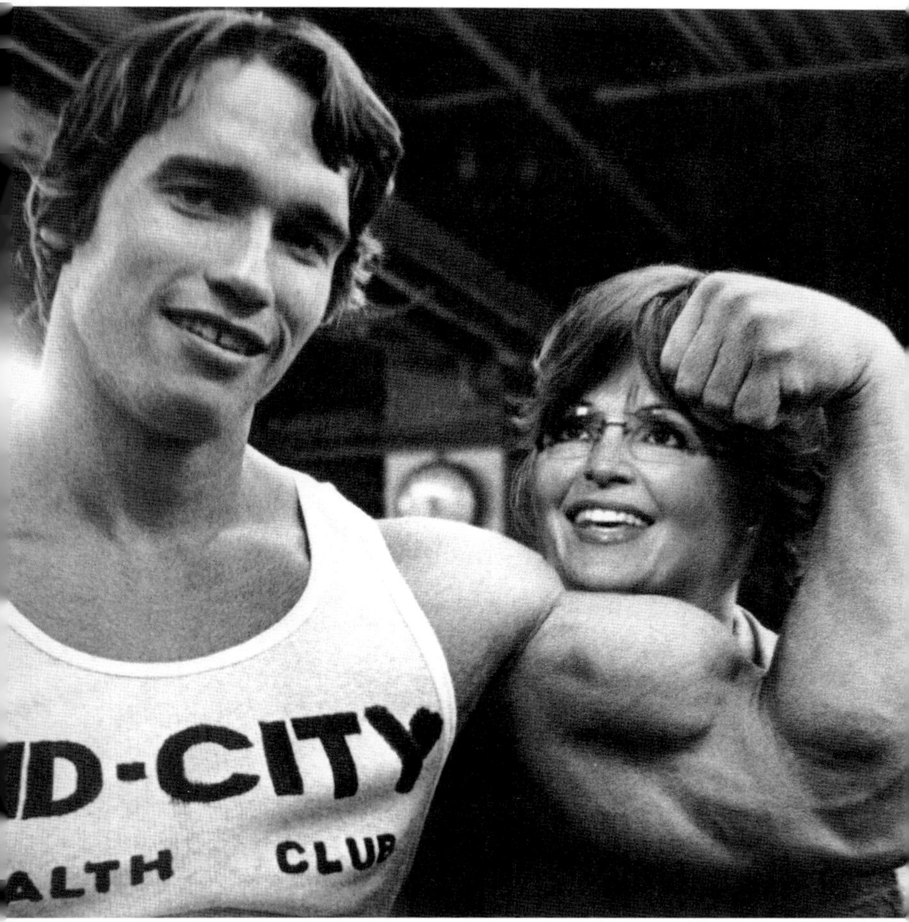
D-CITY
ALTH CLUB

"After weeks of banging heads together at Camp David, we finally forged a lasting peace between Egypt and Israel. Here I am with my good friends Menachem and Anwar celebrating our historic breakthrough. Gosh, I miss those guys!"

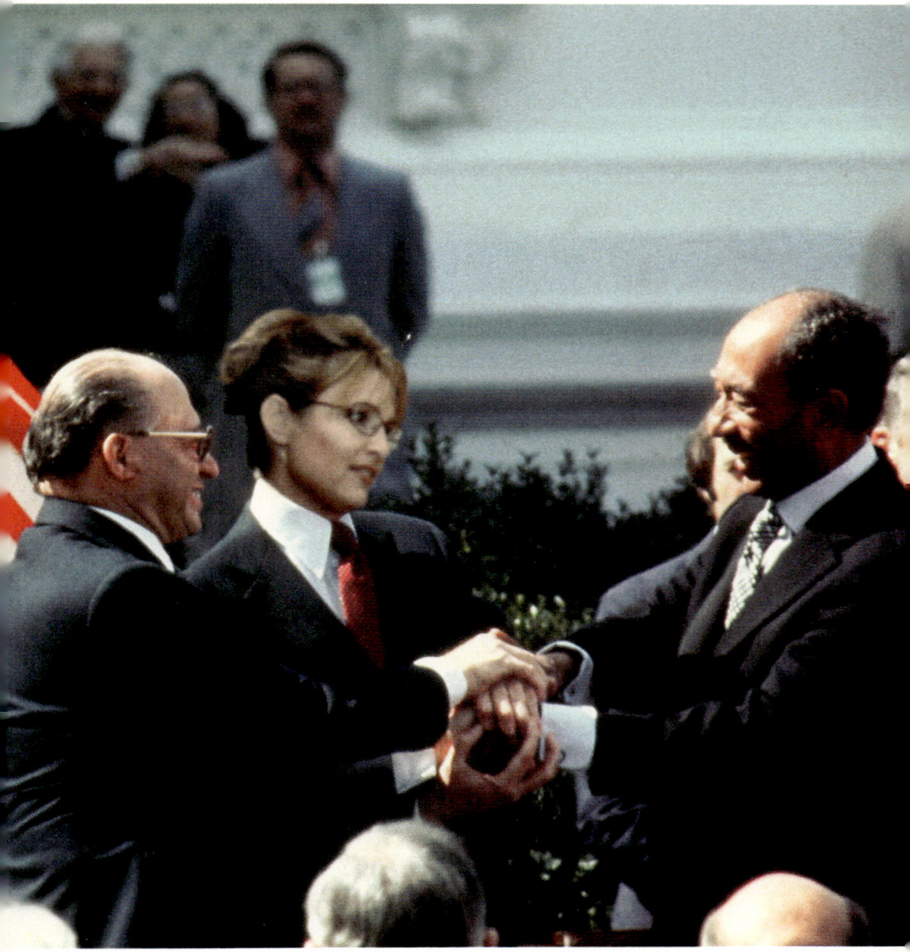

Delivering school report cards by dog sled during one of Alaska's blizzards. Sarah ran for her seat on the Wasilla City Council in 1992, under the slogan "a safer, more progressive Wasilla."

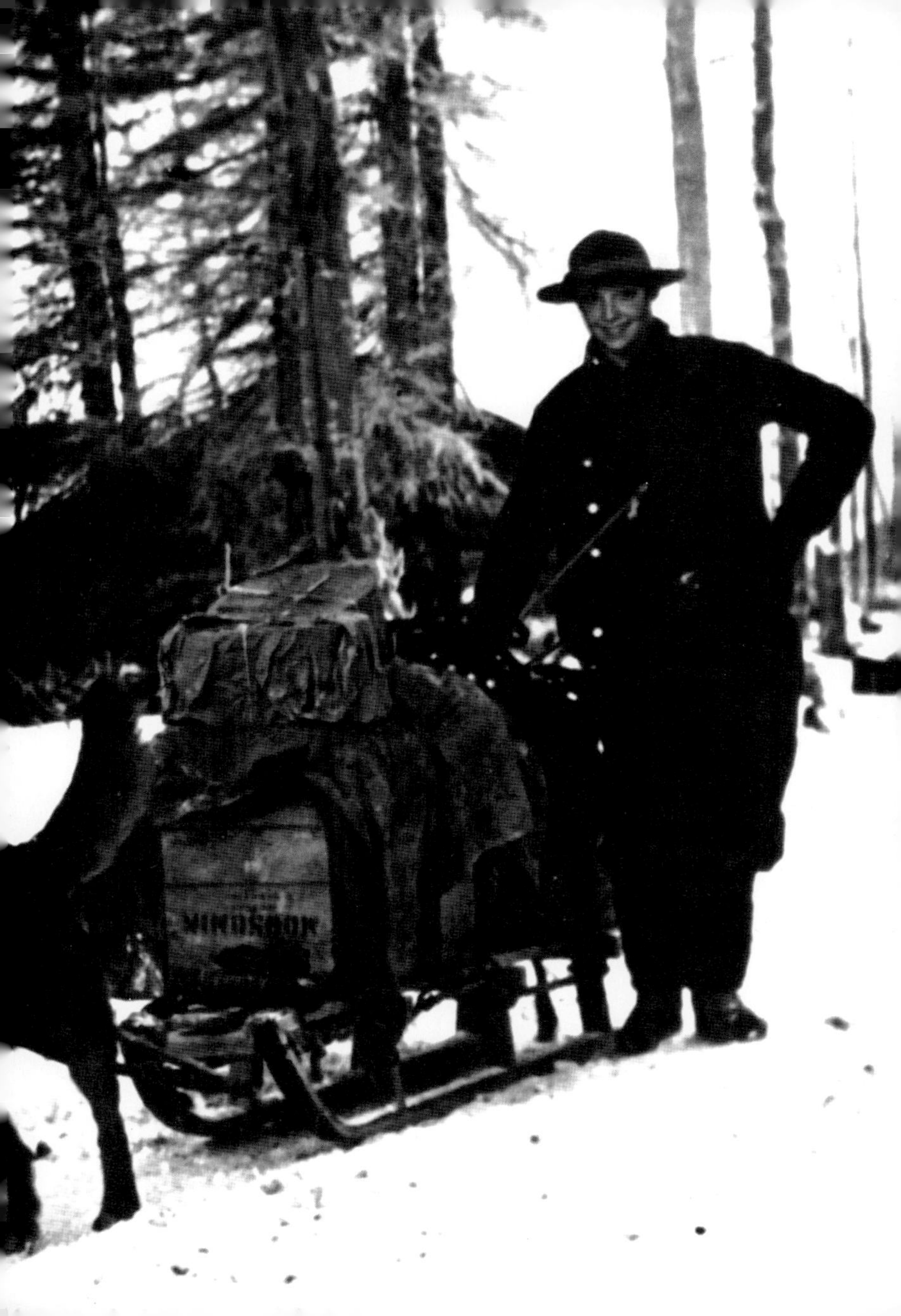

Summers are brief in Alaska, sometimes lasting only a few days. So when the weather permits, Sarah likes to put on her tiara and take a ride around town with the top down.

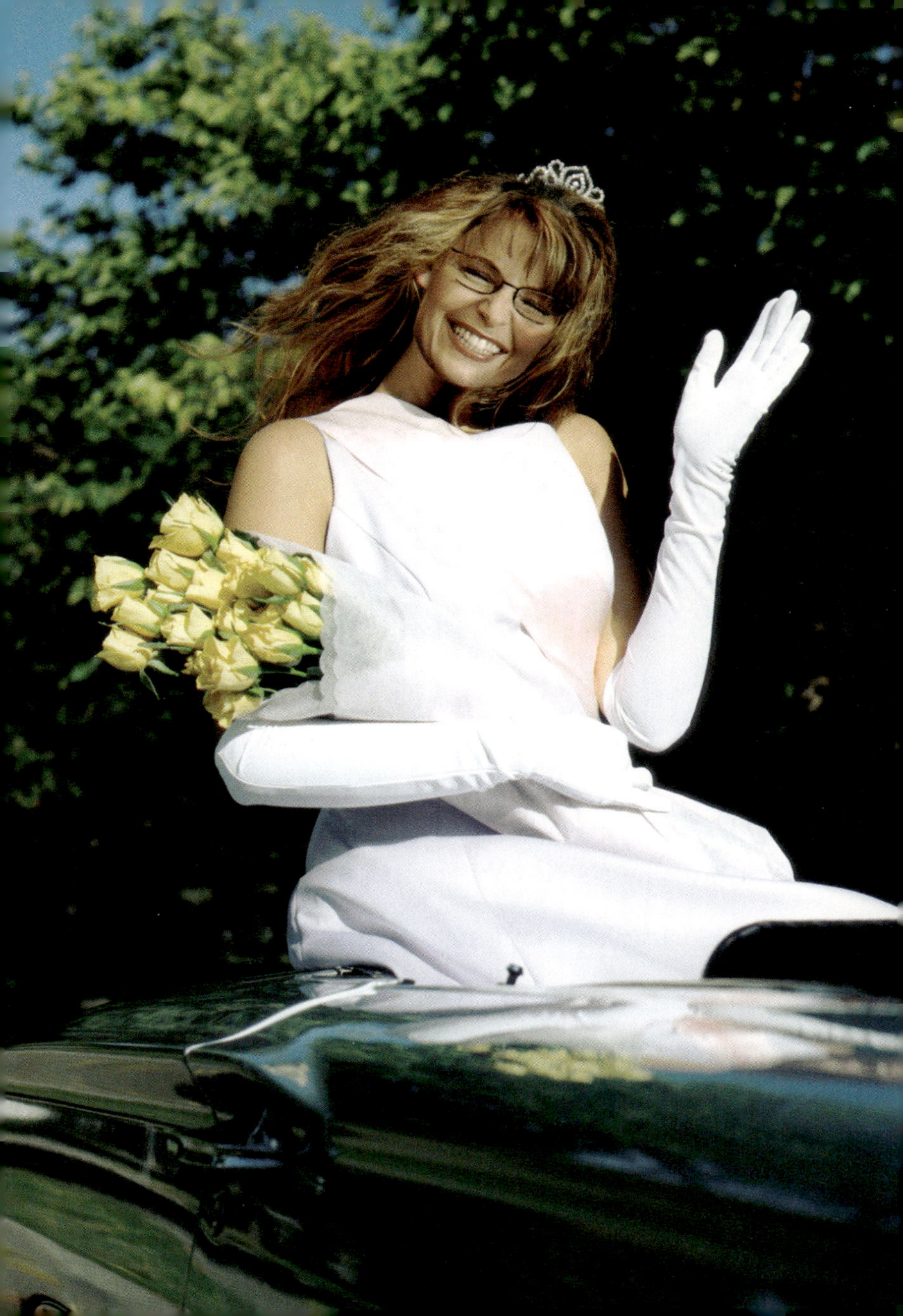

The Iditarod has been called "the last great race on earth": a grueling 1,150-mile odyssey over some of the roughest, most beautiful terrain Alaska has to offer. Only the toughest competitors tackle this demanding course; but Sarah Palin did, and in 1998 she became the third woman in history to win.

Cabela's
WORLD'S FOREMOST OUTFITTER®
31
Cabela's
ALASKA INDUSTRIAL
AIH
HARDWARE, INC.

As we say in Alaska, "Drill, baby, drill!"

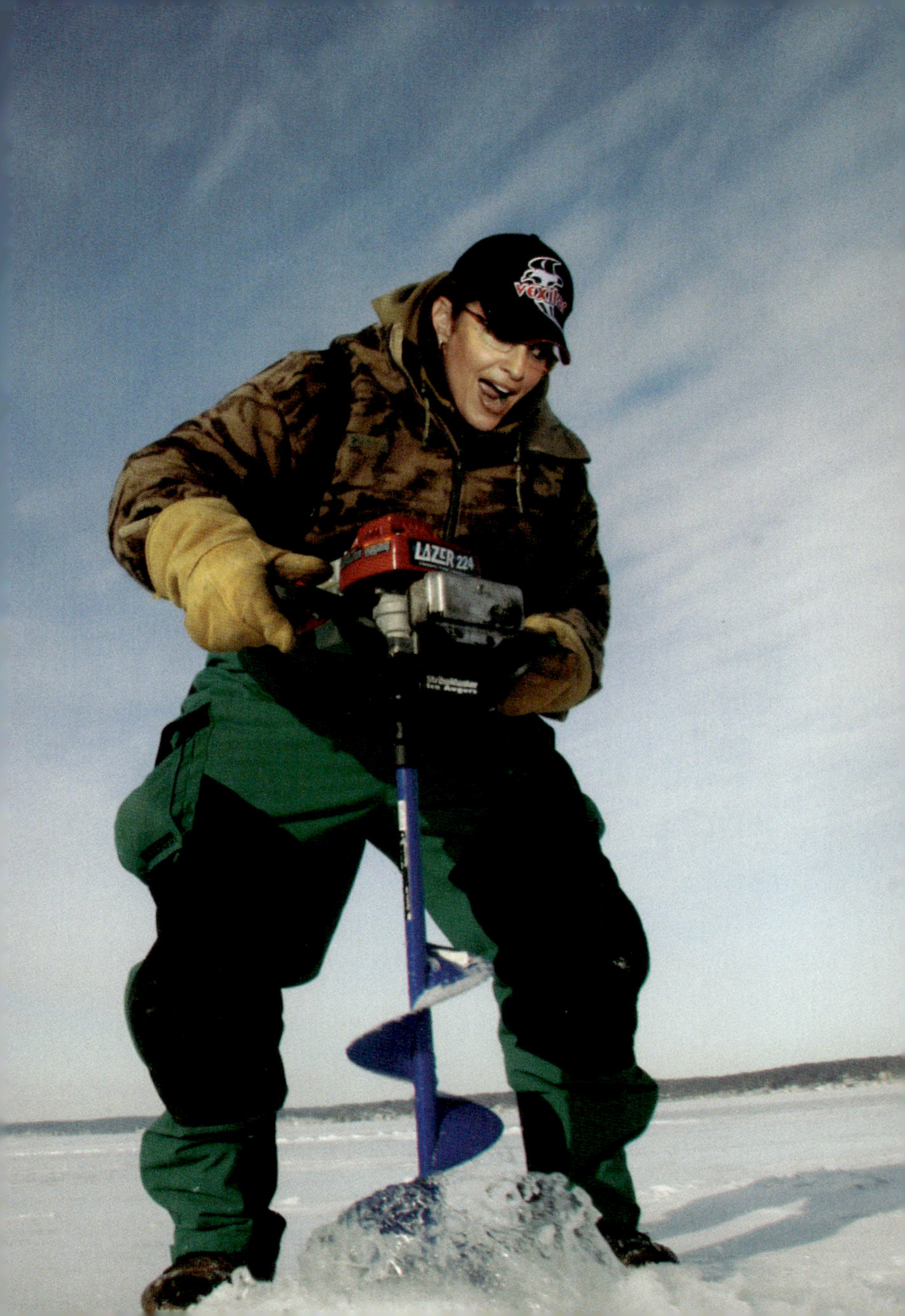
LAZER 224

"Honey, I caught Sunday brunch. Can you bring home the bagels?"

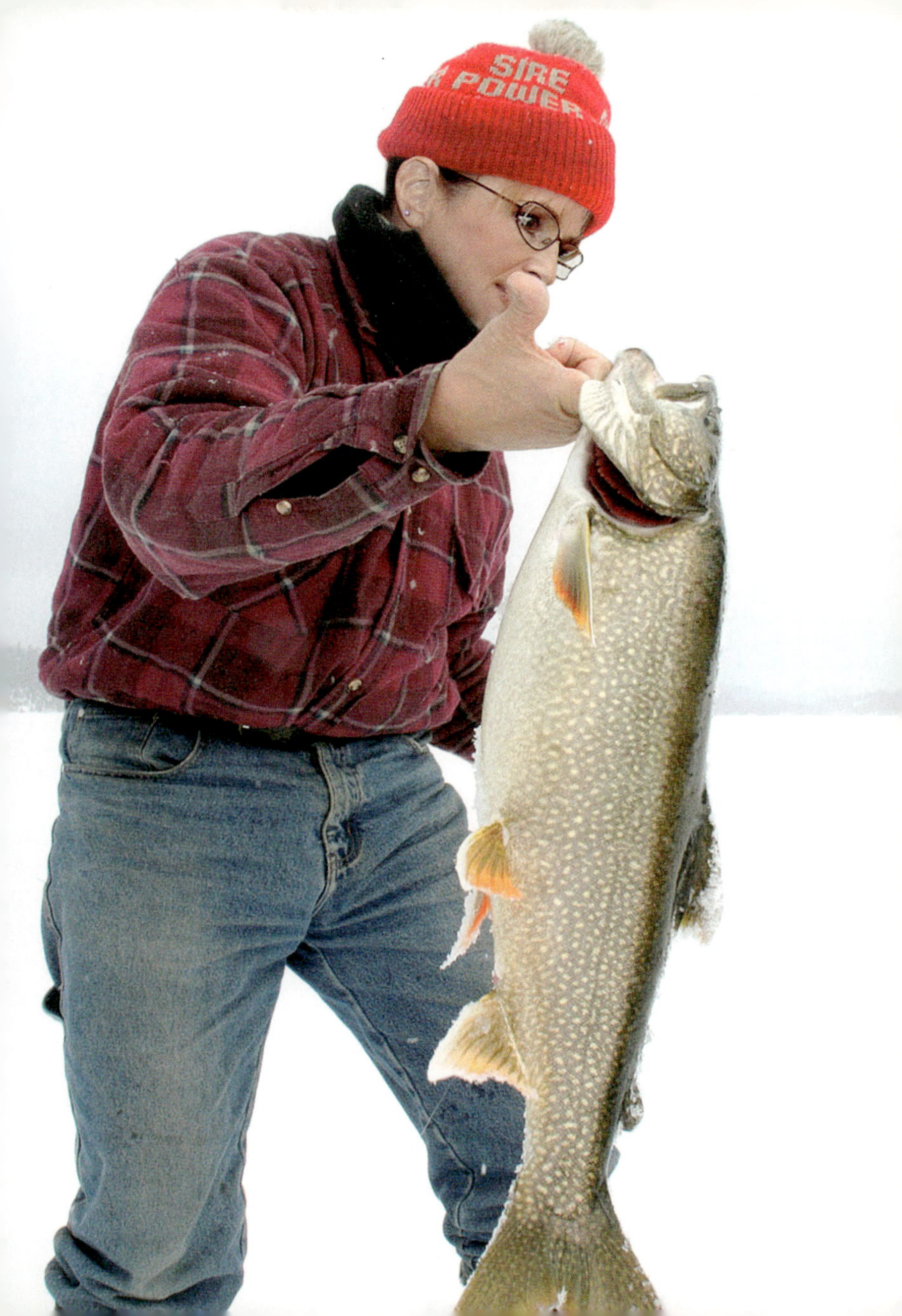
SIRE
POWER

Although she is a charter member of the NRA, Sarah is a true huntress and can bring down her kill with a bow, a slingshot, or a boomerang.

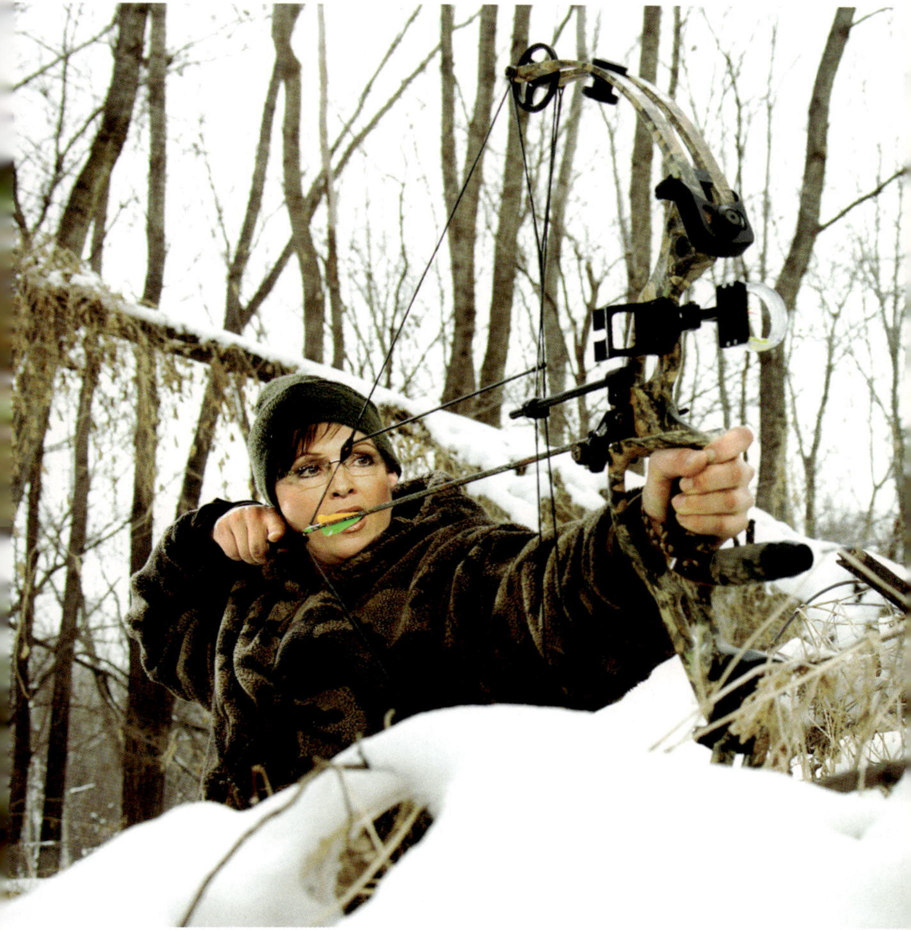

On weekends, Sarah moonlights as a volunteer firefighter in Wasilla.

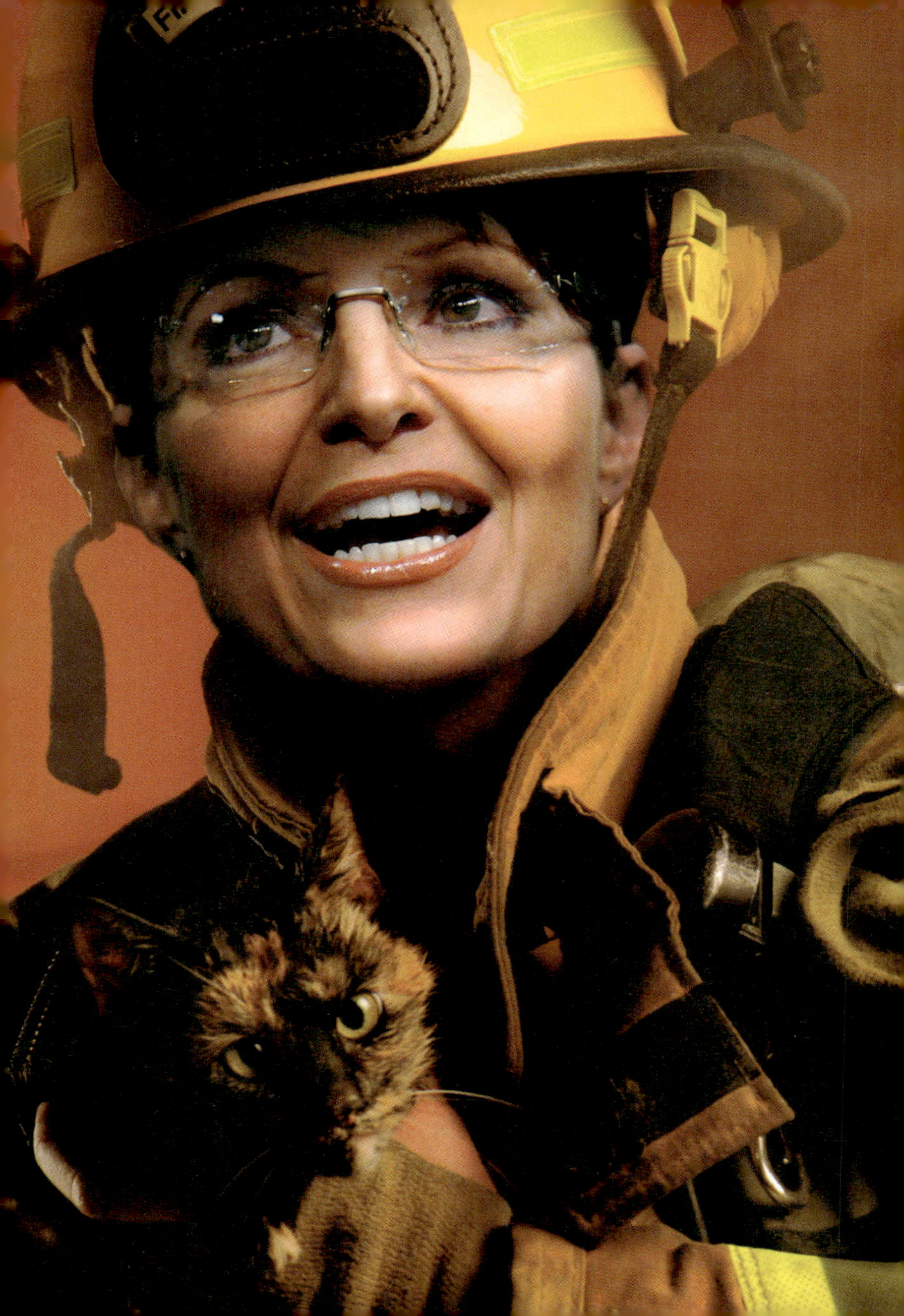

Like many native Alaskans, Sarah spends a lot of her free time in the wild, communing with nature.

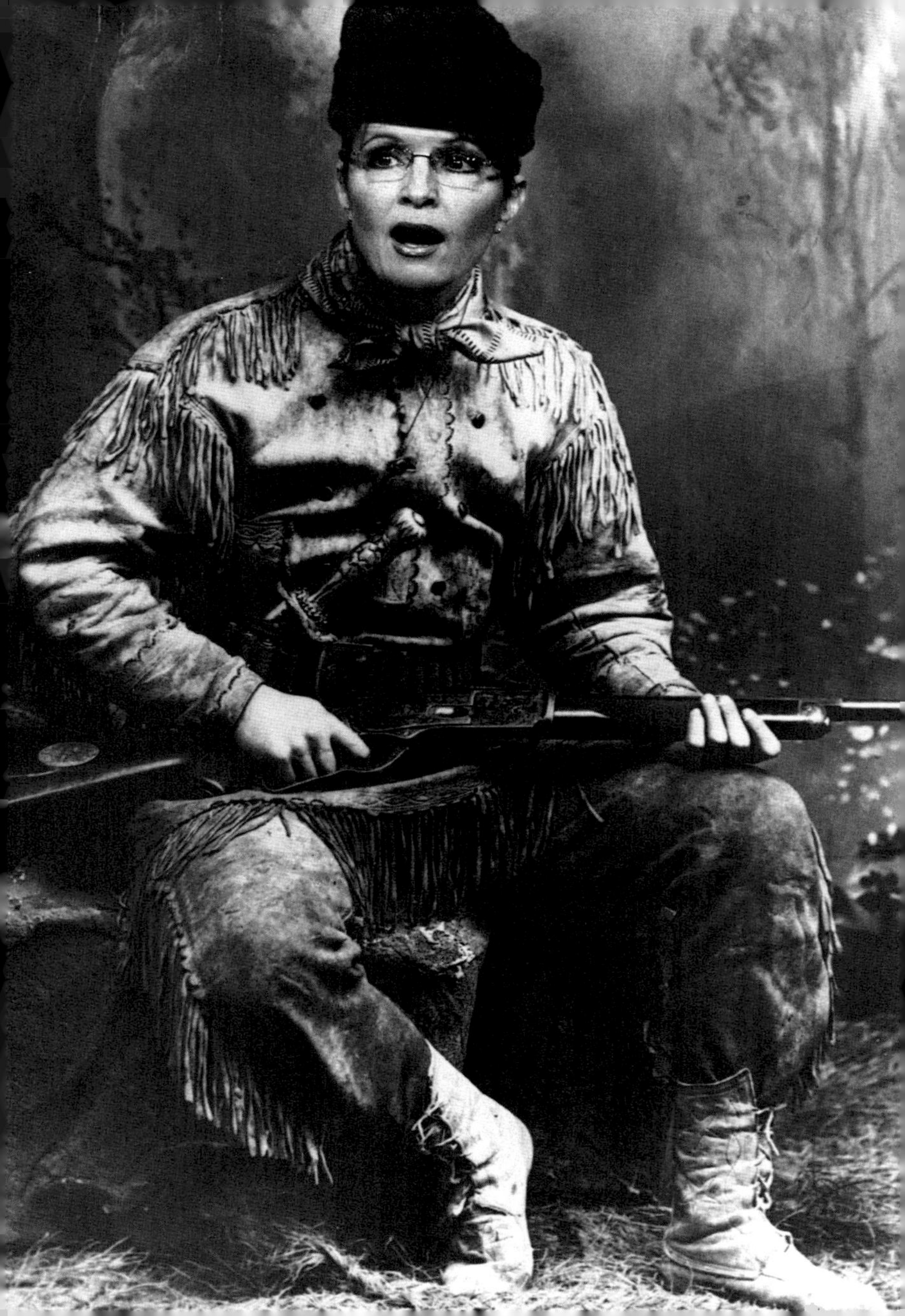

Little known outside the Arctic Circle, curling is a popular winter sport originally played with frozen moose heads. Sarah was three-time state champ.

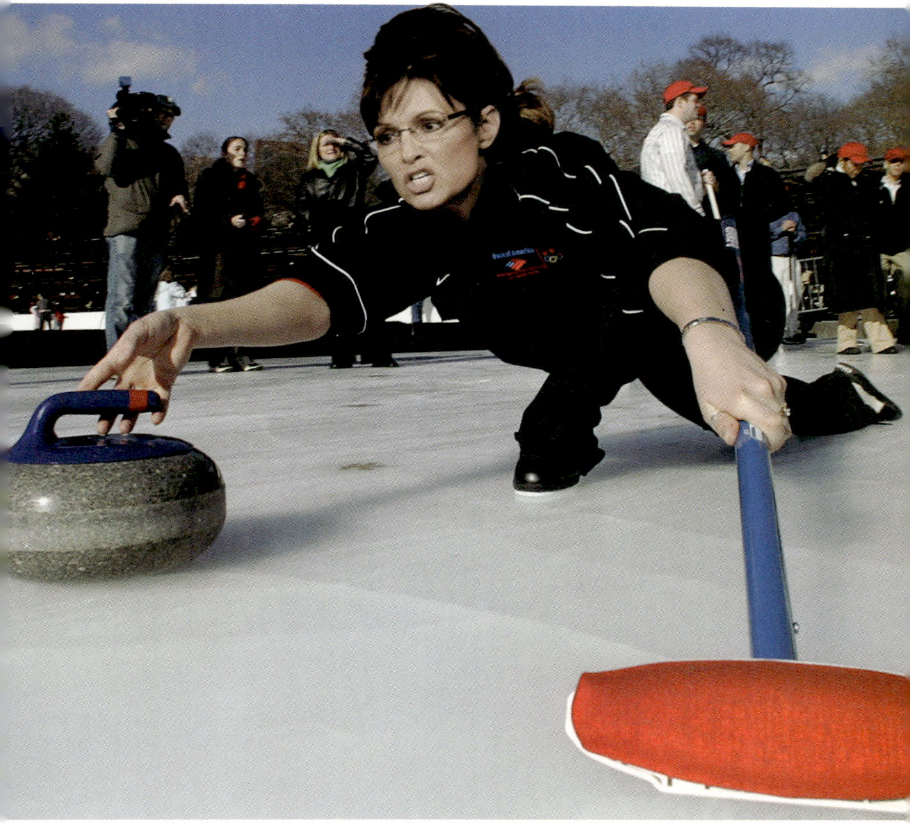

"In addition to my other sporting interests, I also starred on the high school wrestling team. Watch me pin this wolf in 30 seconds!"

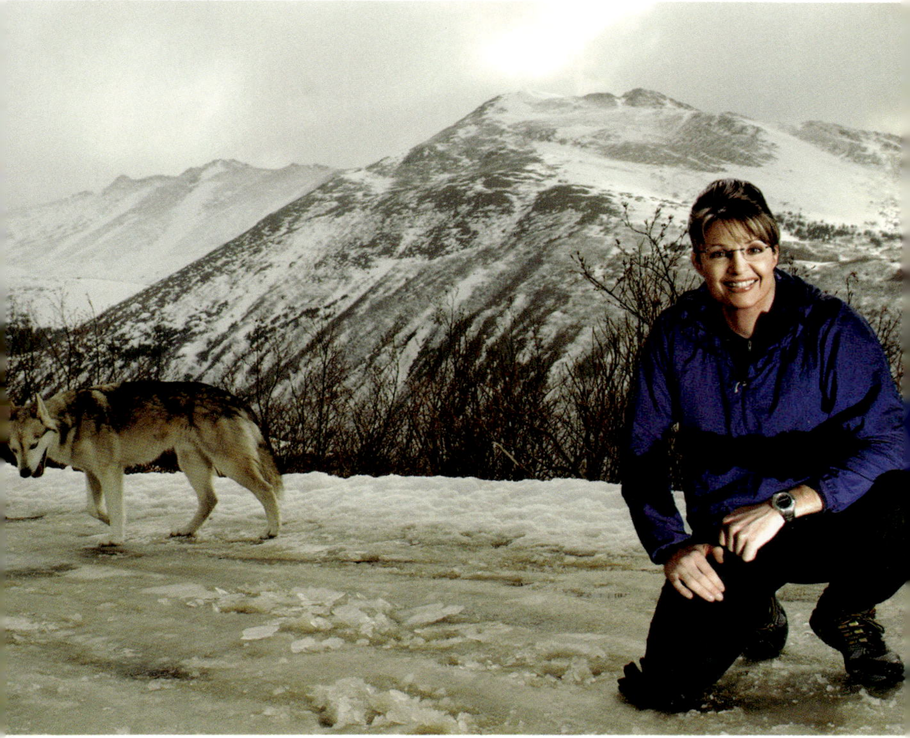

No self-respecting Alaskan can pass up a tree-sawing contest, and Sarah Palin is no exception. Here she is in 2002 during her unsuccessful campaign for lieutenant governor, sawing through a tree trunk the old-fashioned way and in record time.

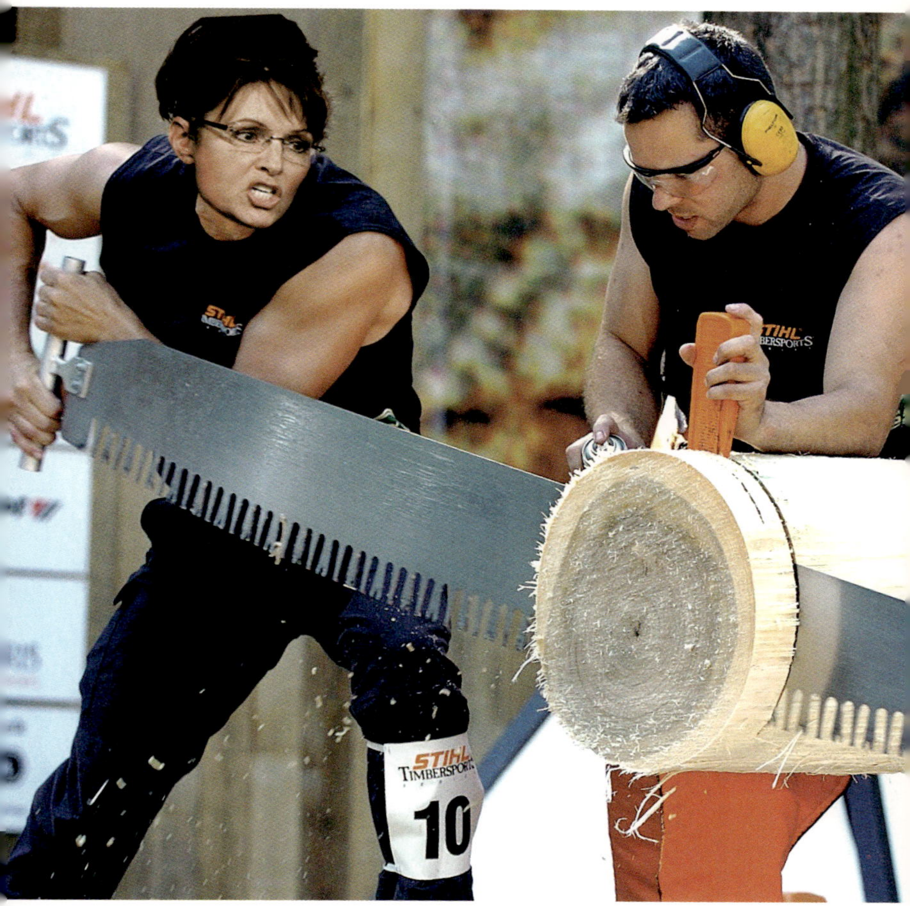

STIHL
TIMBERSPORTS
10
STIHL
TIMBERSPORTS

As Governor, Sarah decided to forgo the trappings of office. Instead of driving to work in a limousine, she rows to work each day in a longboat. Sometimes the ice is pretty thick though.

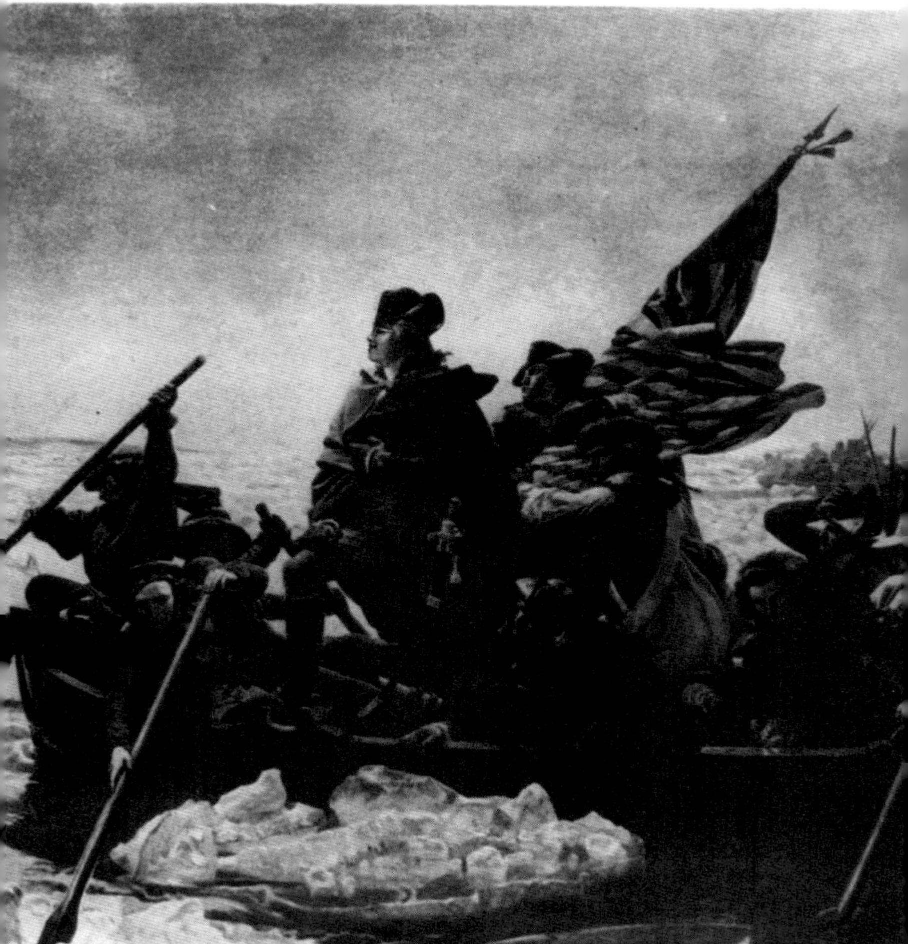

You've heard the expression, "Only Palin can go to China"? Here, the Governor trades recipes with Madame Mao at a performance of the Beijing Ballet.

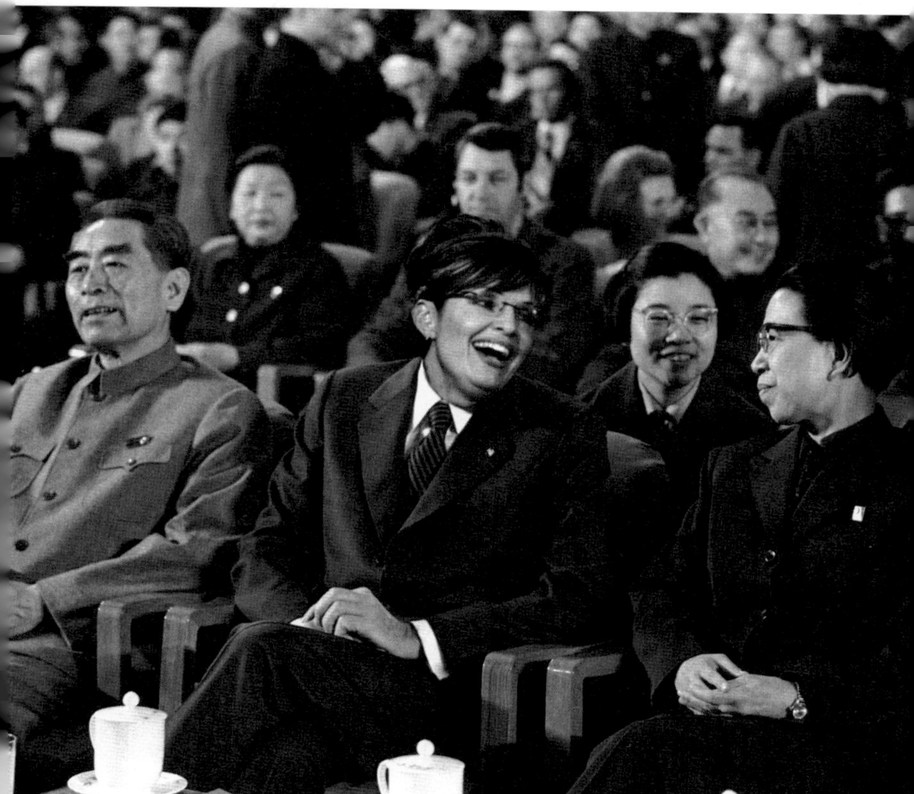

The Governor takes time out between trade and security talks for a quick visit to the Great Wall.

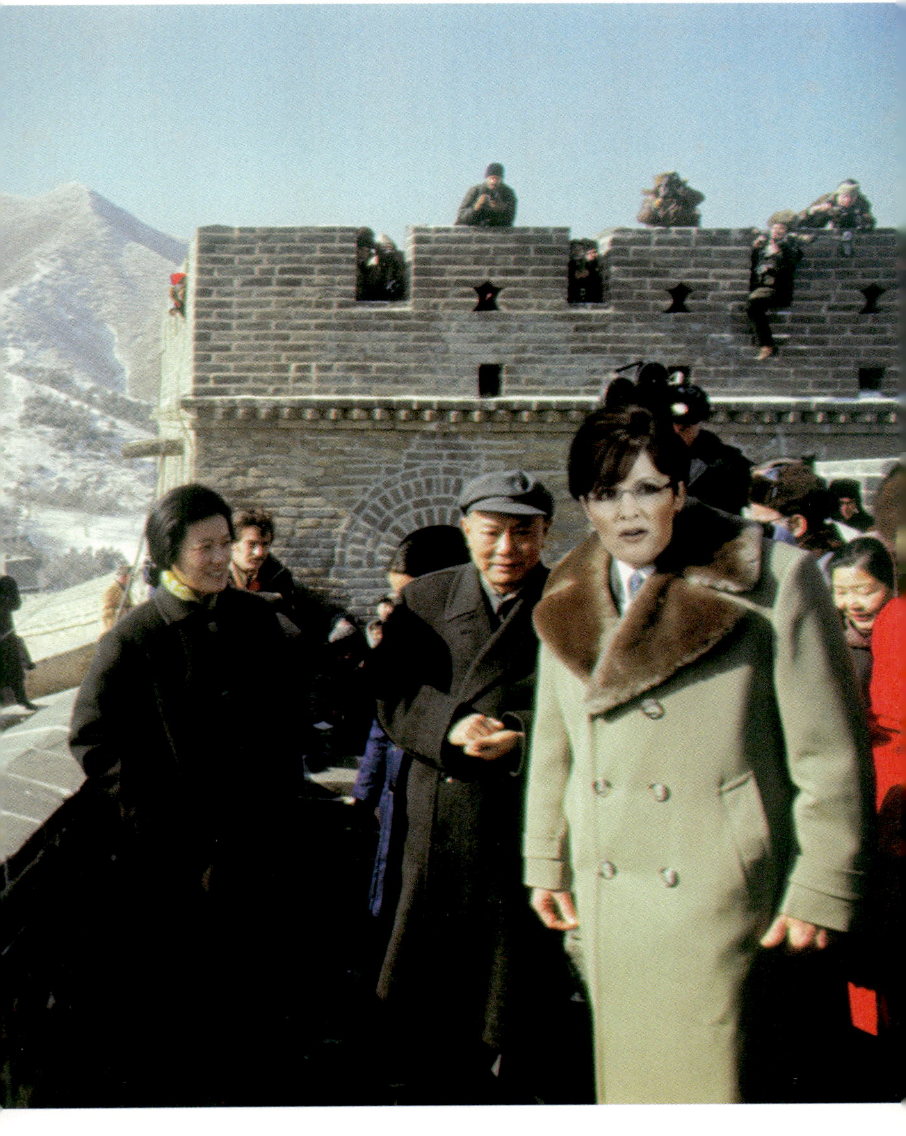

As Governor, Sarah does her part to promote tourism.

HEART OF THE KLONDIKE
WRITTEN BY SCOTT MARBLE.
THE FIRST BIG "FIND".

"This is our walk-in fridge at home. It isn't easy killing enough game to feed a family of seven. Half of these critters are protected species!"

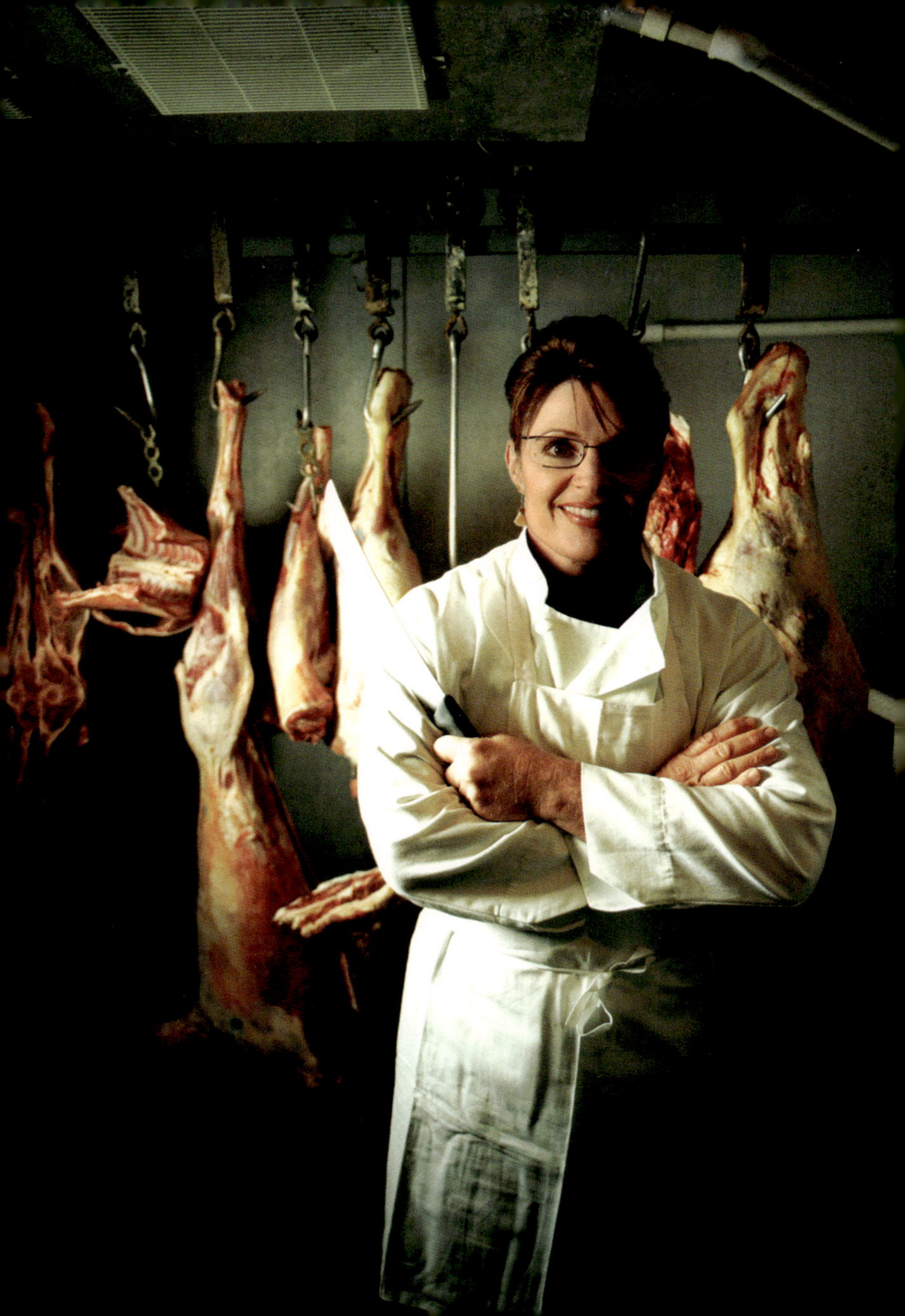

"This is me with the head of Senator Ted Stevens."

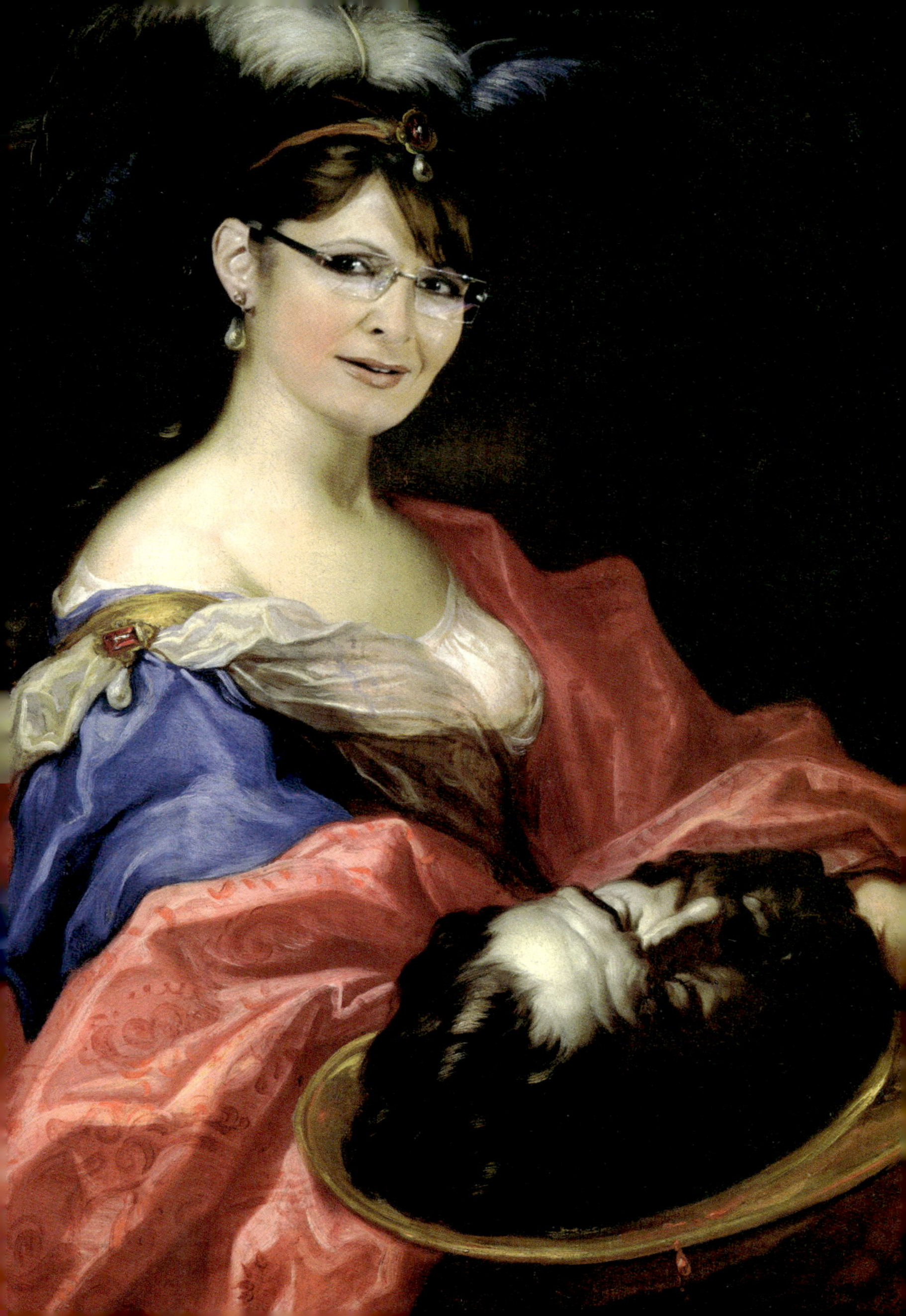

"When John McCain asked me to be his running mate, I said 'Yes!' And I gave him a shiny red apple to show my appreciation."

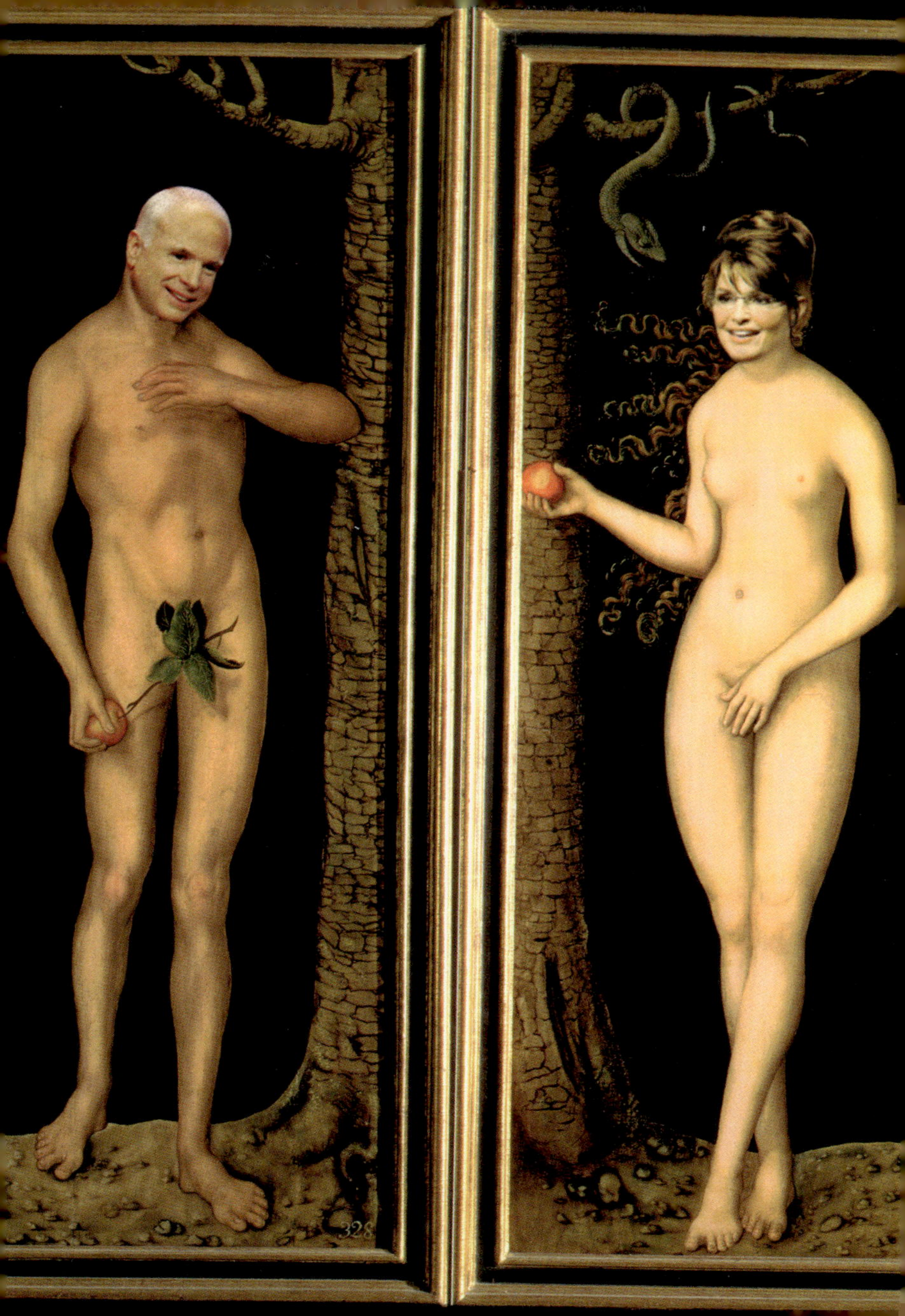
328

"I just want to remind our Democratic friends in Congress that up here in Alaska, we eat what we kill—and then we wear it!"

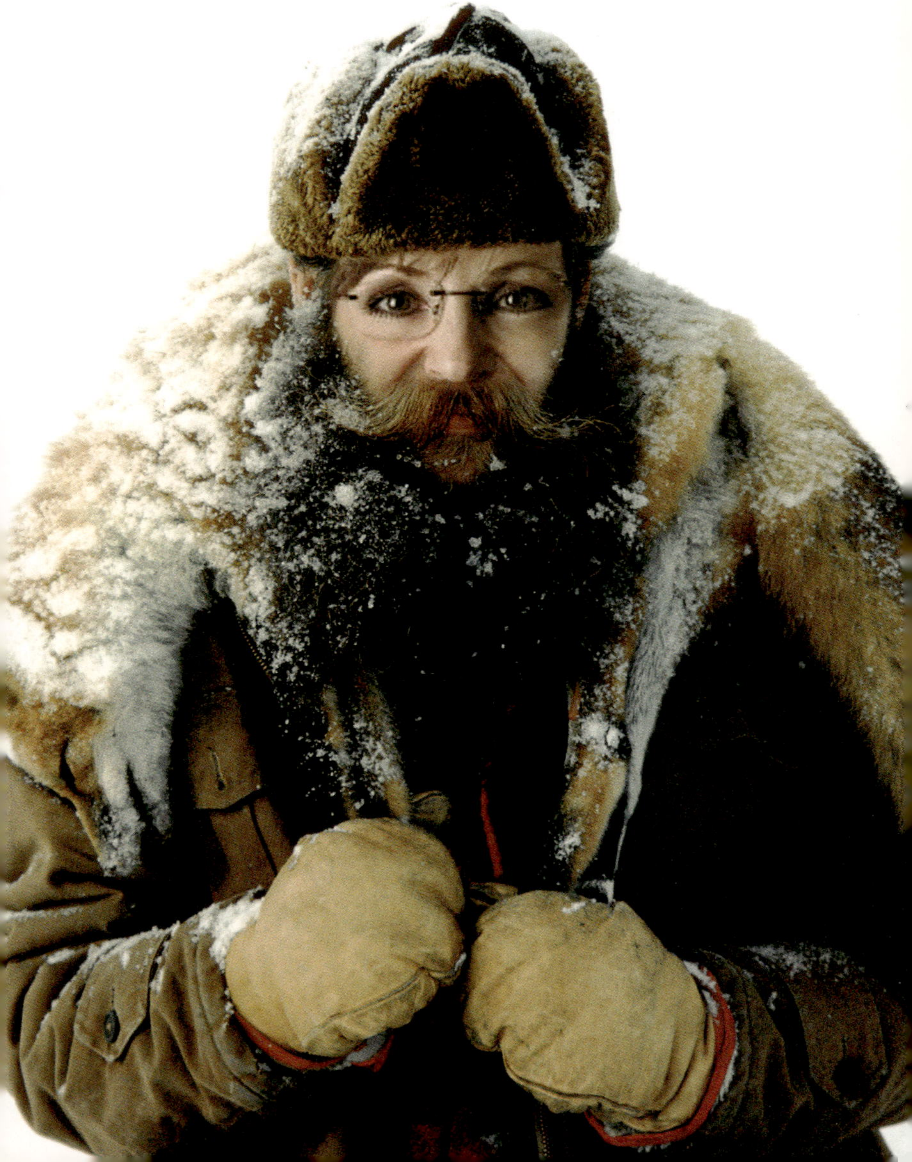

"This is me posing in my inaugural outfit, which I ordered special for the occasion. Do you think the scepters are over the top? Maybe just one?"

"There's no limit to what women can achieve. I'm going to shatter that glass ceiling into a million pieces!"

PICTURE CREDITS

p. 7: Library of Congress; p. 9: © H. Armstrong Roberts/ClassicStock/Corbis; p. 11: © Bettmann/CORBIS; p. 13: © Bettmann/CORBIS; p. 15: Library of Congress; p. 17: Library of Congress; p. 19: Library of Congress; p. 21: Library of Congress; p. 23: Louvre, Paris, France, Lauros / Giraudon /The Bridgeman Art Library International; p. 25: Library of Congress; p. 27: Library of Congress; p. 29: Library of Congress; p. 33: © Glyn Jones /Corbis; p. 35: Library of Congress; p. 37: © Pat Doyle / Corbis; p. 39: Library of Congress; p. 41: © Bettmann/CORBIS; p. 43: Library of Congress; p. 45: Photograph by Abbie Rowe, National Park Service, in the John F. Kennedy Presidential Library and Museum, Boston; p. 47: Library of Congress; p. 49: © Marvy! / CORBIS; p. 51: © Bettmann/CORBIS; p. 55: Library of Congress; p. 57: © Michael Martin / zefa / Corbis; p. 65: © Ron Chapple / Corbis; p. 67: © Don Hammond / Design Pics / Corbis; p. 69: © CORBIS; p. 77: Library of Congress; p. 79: © Bettmann / CORBIS; p. 81: © Bettmann / CORBIS; p. 83: Library of Congress; p. 85: © Ben Fink / Brand X / CORBIS; p. 87: Musee des Beaux-Arts, Valenciennes, France, Lauros / Giraudon / The Bridgeman Art Library International; p. 89: Kunsthistorisches Museum, Vienna, Austria, / The Bridgeman Art Library International; p. 91: © Olivier Martel / Corbis; p. 93: Musee de l'Armee, Paris, France, Giraudon / The Bridgeman Art Library International; p. 95: © Joseph Sohm; Visions of America / CORBIS.

All images have been digitally altered.